Praise for *How To Change*

"A must read for anyone looking to improve their habits—or their life."
—Charles Duhigg, *New York Times*
bestselling author of *The Power of Habit*

"If you're dreaming of a 'new you,' start here."
—Dan Heath, *New York Times* bestselling
coauthor of *Made to Stick* and *Switch*

"Smart, pioneering, and packed with the biggest breakthroughs of our decade."
—Arianna Huffington, founder and CEO, Thrive Global

"Katy Milkman is a wonder. In this book, she shares all her secret sauce."
—Richard H. Thaler, recipient of the Nobel Prize in economics; *New York Times*
bestselling coauthor of *Nudge*

"An invaluable guide to success packed with insights that can help you achieve your
financial and life goals."   —Charles R. Schwab

"This book is like having the smartest friend in the world whispering in your ear.
You'll want to send Katy Milkman a thank-you note."
—Daniel H. Pink, *New York Times* bestselling
author of *When*, *Drive*, and *To Sell Is Human*

"A masterful tour of how behavior change works."
—David Epstein, *New York Times* bestselling author of *Range*

"Everyone wants to know: What makes personal change happen and stick? Milkman uses the latest science to give us answers."
—Carol S. Dweck, *New York Times* bestselling author of *Mindset*

"If you want to master tailored, science-based strategies for overcoming obstacles,
read this engaging book."   —Eric Schmidt, former CEO of Google

"An extraordinary roadmap for overcoming the greatest challenge of all—becoming
who we believe we should be."
—General Stanley McChrystal, U.S. Army (retired),
New York Times bestselling author of *Team of Teams* and *Leaders*

"This book is a triple threat: evidence-based, engrossing, and full of effective strategies for making smarter choices."
—Adam Grant, *New York Times* bestselling author
of *Think Again*; host of the TED podcast *WorkLife*

"If your goal is to get better, or to make your teams or business better, READ
THIS BOOK."
—Laszlo Bock, CEO, Humu; former senior vice-president of people,
Google; *New York Times* bestselling author of *Work Rules!*

"A healthy lifestyle is not illusive; this book is a must read to understand the path to
create lasting change."   —Tony Ueber, CEO, 24 Hour Fitness

"Brilliant. Personal. And best of all, actionable. A highlight reel of what scientists know about how to change behavior for good."

—Angela Duckworth, *New York Times* bestselling author of *Grit*

"Katy Milkman does a masterful job of translating science to action."

—Gary Foster, chief scientific officer, WW

"A remarkably useful survey of the behavior change revolution. Milkman tells us what works, what doesn't, and why."

—Stephen J. Dubner, *New York Times* bestselling coauthor of *Freakonomics*; host of *Freakonomics Radio*

"You owe it to yourself to read this book from cover to cover."

—Steve D. Levitt, *New York Times* bestselling coauthor of *Freakonomics*

"Katy Milkman not only delivers the most cutting edge science on change, she also makes you feel like she is by your side cheering you on. A must read for anyone who wants to remake their life for the better."

—Annie Duke, bestselling author of *Thinking in Bets* and *How to Decide*

"This is your chance. When you're ready to change, when you are committed to change, this delightful book will help you turn your intentions into reality."

—Seth Godin, author of *This Is Marketing*

"Plenty of books offer advice on how to overcome common personal barriers but none as clearly, engagingly, and compellingly as this."

—Robert Cialdini, *New York Times* bestselling author of *Influence* and *Pre-Suasion*

"Packed with clever insights, cool experiments, and deep science, this book is engaging, important, and oh-so valuable."

—Nicholas A. Christakis, MD, PhD, *New York Times* bestselling author of *Blueprint* and *Apollo's Arrow*

"From this book, you will not only gain insight into your own behavior, but will be inspired to create your own fresh start."

—Wendy Wood, author of *Good Habits, Bad Habits*

"A much-needed, easy-to-follow instruction manual for understanding what stops you from achieving your personal goals and how you can do better."

—Laurie Santos, host of *The Happiness Lab*

"This extraordinary guide left me with that magical feeling that change is possible."

—Dolly Chugh, author of *The Person You Mean to Be*; Jacob B. Melnick Term Professor, NYU Stern School of Business

"You will learn, grow, and be inspired by the personal accounts and engaging research highlighting the science of behavior change. This book is a must read!"

—Modupe Akinola, associate professor of management, Columbia Business School; host of *TED Business*

HOW
TO
CHANGE

PORTFOLIO / PENGUIN

HOW

TO

CHANGE

The Science of Getting
from Where You Are
to Where You Want to Be

Katy Milkman

Foreword by Angela Duckworth

Portfolio/Penguin
An imprint of Penguin Random House LLC
penguinrandomhouse.com

Most Portfolio books are available at a discount when purchased in quantity for sales promotions or corporate use. Special editions, which include personalized covers, excerpts, and corporate imprints, can be created when purchased in large quantities. For more information, please call (212) 572-2232 or e-mail specialmarkets@penguinrandomhouse.com. Your local bookstore can also assist with discounted bulk purchases using the Penguin Random House corporate Business-to-Business program. For assistance in locating a participating retailer, e-mail B2B@penguinrandomhouse.com.

LIBRARY OF CONGRESS CATALOGING-IN-PUBLICATION DATA
Names: Milkman, Katherine L., author.
Title: How to Change : The Science of Getting from Where You
Are to Where You Want to Be / Katy Milkman ; foreword by Angela Duckworth.
Description: [New York] : Portfolio/Penguin, an imprint of Penguin
Random House LLC, [2021] | Includes bibliographical references and index.
Identifiers: LCCN 2021006495 | ISBN 9780593083758 (hardcover) |
ISBN 9780593332597 (international edition) | ISBN 9780593083765 (ebook)
Subjects: LCSH: Change (Psychology) | Self-actualization (Psychology) |
Behavior modification.
Classification: LCC BF637.C4 M54 2021 | DDC 158.1—dc23
LC record available at https://lccn.loc.gov/2021006495

Printed in the United States of America

Book design by Cassandra Garruzzo

*This book is dedicated to the two families
that made my scientific career possible:*

*First, to my husband, Cullen; my son, Cormac;
and my parents, Bev and Ray*

*Second, to my academic family: my mentor, Max; my fellow
Max advisees and collaborators, John, Todd, Dolly, and Modupe;
my current partner in crime, Angela; and my mentees, Hengchen,
Edward, Erika, and Aneesh*

Contents

Foreword

Before I met Katy in person, here's what I'd heard from colleagues who knew her well.

"Smartest person you'll ever meet."

"Crazy productive. Will make you feel like a slacker."

"A machine. I mean, what I do in a week, she does in a day."

What sort of superhuman is Katy Milkman?

Because I now count myself among her awestruck colleagues, I can tell you that in many ways, Katy *is* the smartest person I've ever met, by far the most productive, and yes, what she is able to accomplish, by comparison, does make me feel like I'm moving in slow motion.

But Katy is not, in fact, superhuman. Instead, she is what you and I aspire to be, and what she shows us in this book all of us can be: a *super* human.

By that I mean that Katy Milkman is a master of human nature. She has figured out how to line up her actions with her goals and dreams. Her first attempts—at anything—may not be perfect, but literally whatever Katy cares about, she quickly learns how to do better and better, faster and faster, and more and more efficiently. And as a world-renowned behavioral scientist who has spent her entire career on these questions, she understands how hard it can be to be human, and how we can all do a better job of it, at the deepest level.

Though it wasn't obvious at the beginning of our friendship, I now see that Katy copes with the same fallibilities we all share. She wants to eat cookies and potato chips instead of apples and spinach. She'd rather procrastinate than get back to work. She is capable of anger and impatience.

An engineer by training and by temperament, Katy approaches any of these challenges as problems to be solved. And it is that mindset, I think, that makes Katy such a *super* human.

In other words, what Katy has learned is that the secret to a better life is not to eradicate the impulses that make us human but instead to understand them, outsmart them, and whenever possible, to make them work for us rather than against us.

For me, the lessons Katy has to share have improved my life enormously. I get in my ten thousand steps more often. I write emails more quickly. In a thousand ways, she has helped me find hacks to make my life easier and better.

Many of the lessons Katy shares in this book grew out of the work we do together at the Behavior Change for Good Initiative—an ambitious project we've led for the past five years, investigating what it takes to change habits. We've studied new ways to increase daily gym attendance, charitable giving, vaccination rates, and student achievement, and we've developed new methods for advancing the science of behavior change. But two people could never tackle such a challenging question alone, so Katy and I have assembled a team of more than a hundred leading intellectuals from around the world, each trained in different traditions, including economics, medicine, law, psychology, sociology, neuroscience, and computer science. In this book, you'll learn not only about Katy's work and our work together, but also about the work of our many remarkable collaborators.

Every book is like a conversation with its author. So you have to be picky about the books you read. With your limited time, you want a conversation partner who can teach you something you didn't know. And you want to *like* the person with whom you're in dialogue. You want to enjoy your time together. You want to know they really have your best interests at heart.

And that is why you should keep reading this book, all the way to its end. Undoubtedly, you are like most people I know in that you are trying to change one habit or another for the better. Quite likely, you've attempted to change in the past, repeatedly. You've wondered, *Why is it so very hard to get from where I am to where I want to be?*

In these pages, Katy will teach you things you didn't know. You'll learn how important it is to get the timing right for kick-starting a new habit. You'll learn that forgetting is the silent killer of even our most ardent resolutions. You'll learn that making hard things seem fun is a much better strategy than making hard things seem important.

And most important, throughout the entire conversation, you'll hear Katy asking you, with warmth and humor and a healthy sense of her own limitations, as well as a masterful understanding of human motivation and behavior: "What's your problem?"

You'll feel like she truly cares about helping you change. You'll feel like you're friends with a world-class behavioral scientist who is walking by your side, helping you understand yourself better, and helping you, too, become a *super* human.

You'll try out some of the ideas she suggests. You'll wonder why you hadn't thought of them before Katy suggested them. And you'll learn an approach to life that will generate strategies that even Katy hasn't thought of yet.

One day, people just getting to know you may wonder whether you are somehow immune to the impulses and conflicts that beset normal people. They may compliment you on your crazy productivity. They may ask you for your advice on how to get more done in a day.

And you may choose to introduce them to your friend Katy. "Read this," you'll say with a knowing smile. "We all struggle to line up what we do with what we want. I did, too. Then I learned how to see every impasse in my life as a specific problem to be solved."

You'll assure them that the secret to a better life is not to be superhuman, without desires and quirks and vulnerabilities, but instead to be a problem solver, equipped with the latest scientific knowledge.

I truly believe that this book could be a fresh start for you. I'm so happy you're ready to begin.

Angela Duckworth

HOW

TO

CHANGE

Introduction

I t was early 1994 and Andre Agassi's tennis career was veering dangerously off track. All his life, Agassi had been assured he would go down in history as one of the greats of his sport. When he turned pro at age sixteen in 1986, pundits lauded him for his natural talent, impressed by his uncanny ability to take control of points and his gift for hitting seemingly impossible shots on defense. But by 1994 it wasn't a stellar record on the court that had won Agassi fame—it was his style. In a sport known for decorum, Agassi wore ripped jeans and tie-dyed shirts to tournaments. He grew his hair long and sported an earring. He cursed like a sailor on the court. He even starred in a splashy ad campaign for Canon with the provocative slogan "Image Is Everything."

When it came to tennis, though, Agassi was falling laughably short of expectations. He too often lost early in tournaments to players with far less skill—a first-round flameout at a small tune-up in Germany, a third-round defeat at a Grand Slam. His ranking kept slipping, from seventh in the world to twenty-second, then to thirty-first. Agassi's coach of ten years had recently and unceremoniously dropped him; Agassi learned the news while reading *USA Today*. He'd taken to telling people he hated tennis.

Agassi needed a change.

Which is why he found himself eating dinner one evening at Porto Cervo, a favorite restaurant of his near Miami, across from Brad Gilbert, a fellow pro tennis player. Gilbert's approach to tennis was the polar opposite of Agassi's: fastidious, methodical, and inelegant. He lacked Agassi's obvious gift for the game. And yet Gilbert, then thirty-two years old, had been ranked among the world's top twenty players for years, even reaching number four in 1990, much to the surprise of tennis aficionados. Just a few months before the dinner with Agassi, Gilbert had detailed his unusual approach to tennis in an instant bestseller called *Winning Ugly*.

It was *Winning Ugly* that had prompted the dinner. After reading the book, Agassi's manager had encouraged his struggling client to talk with Gilbert. Agassi needed a new coach, and his manager had a hunch that Gilbert, who was old enough to consider retiring from the pro tour, might be the person who could turn Agassi's career around. Agassi had agreed to the meeting, but as he would later recount in his brilliant 2009 autobiography, *Open*, he was skeptical. Gilbert was known for his peculiarities, both on and off the court, and as the dinner unfolded, he only added to Agassi's uncertainty. First, Gilbert refused an outdoor seat with an ocean view (citing a mosquito phobia). Then, upon discovering his favorite beer wasn't on the menu, he dashed to a nearby market to pick up a six-pack and insisted it be stored on ice in the restaurant's freezer.

It took a while for the group to get settled but when they finally did, Agassi's manager opened with a question for Gilbert. What, he asked, did Gilbert think of his client's game? Gilbert took a long swig of his drink and swallowed slowly. He didn't mince words. If he had Agassi's skills and talent, he replied, he'd be dominating the pro tour. As he saw it, Agassi was misusing his gifts: "You try to hit a winner on every ball," he said. It was a serious shortcoming. No one can hit an outright winner on every shot, Gilbert pointed out, and trying to do so was eroding Agassi's confidence bit by bit each time he fell short. Having played against (and beaten) Agassi many times, Gilbert had witnessed this pattern firsthand.

Agassi could see the wisdom in this assessment. He'd always been a perfectionist, but until Gilbert's remarks, he'd viewed that trait as a strength rather than a weakness. Growing up, he'd learned to go for the kill from his father, an Olympic boxer who was perpetually hunting for the knockout blow—the one punch that would vanquish his opponent. During training sessions on the homemade court in their backyard, the Olympian had echoed the advice of his former boxing coach. "Hit *harder*!" he'd yell at his five-year-old son. "Hit earlier!" Agassi had long considered his exceptional ability to hit knockout shots an advantage. Gilbert was saying it was his Achilles' heel.

To win, Gilbert continued, Agassi needed to shift his focus. "Stop thinking about yourself," he admonished, "and remember that the guy on the other side of the net has weaknesses." It was Gilbert's uncanny ability to size up his opponents that allowed him to beat far better players. He didn't try for a knockout to claim each point; he found a strategy that eased that burden. "Instead of you succeeding," Gilbert said, "make him fail. Better yet, *let* him fail."

Because Agassi was looking to hit a perfect shot every time, Gilbert explained, he was "stacking the odds against" himself and "assuming too much risk."

Gilbert's message was simple: the self-focused approach to tennis on which Agassi had built his career was not the best approach—not if he wanted to win. There was a better way—one that required sizing up the competition and tailoring his game to capitalize on his opponents' weaknesses. It might be a less dazzling style of tennis than Agassi was used to playing, but it would be more effective.

Fifteen minutes into the conversation, Gilbert got up to use the restroom. Agassi immediately turned to his manager. "That's our guy," he said.

A few months later, Agassi entered the U.S. Open unseeded—he wasn't even expected to crack the top sixteen. But with Gilbert's coaching, his style had changed. He faced an old rival early on—the tournament's sixth seed, Michael Chang—and remained unshaken in a nail-biter, holding on to the win by the thinnest of margins. He took out the ninth seed with ease, recognizing his opponent's "tell"—a tendency to look at the spot where he planned to hit his serves—and exploiting that weakness.

And, suddenly, Agassi had reached the finals. There was 550,000 dollars in prize money on the line, but far more in pride. It was Agassi's chance to prove himself—to show everyone that he could live up to the hype after all.

His opponent was Michael Stich, a German champion and the tournament's number four seed. Agassi came out strong, hitting crisp, clean balls on point after point. He won the first set handily, then eked out the second set in a tiebreaker. But Stich wasn't ready to fold. In the third set he hung with Agassi on long rallies and made him work for every point; eventually, the set was tied at five games apiece. The most direct path to victory would require Agassi to break serve, which meant besting Stich when he had the advantage of beginning each point.

Agassi's confidence began to waver. Stich wasn't giving up—he kept blasting powerful serves, one after another. But then Agassi noticed Stich gripping his side, the telltale sign of a cramp, and saw his opening. He broke Stich's serve. He was four points away from winning his first U.S. Open Championship—the sweetest of possible victories for a struggling onetime phenom whom the oddsmakers had counted out.

Before hiring Gilbert, Agassi was notorious for falling apart in high-pressure matches. He went for too many knockouts, took too many risks, and blew it when he should have held steady. But now Agassi stayed focused. Instead of going for winners, he concentrated on keeping the ball in play. He could hear Gilbert's voice in his head: "Go for his forehand. When in doubt, forehand, forehand, forehand." And he stayed on task. He hit the ball over and over again to Stich's forehand, his feeblest shot. And on match point, Stich missed.

The tournament was over. Agassi fell to his knees with tears in his eyes. He was the first unseeded player to take home a U.S. Open trophy in twenty-eight years. He'd made history.

• • •

If you've ever tried to make a big change to your life—to accomplish more at work or in school, to get in shape for a marathon, to build a nest egg for retirement—then you know there's a lot of advice out there about how to succeed. In fact, you've probably tried acting on some of it. Maybe you've tracked your steps with a Fitbit or set calendar reminders on your phone to practice deep-breathing exercises on your lunch break. Perhaps you've cut out your afternoon coffee habit, putting the money you would have spent at the café into a savings account. You know your goals should be specific and measurable. You know the power of positive thinking and incremental progress. You know it's helpful to have a support group.

Thanks to a booming popular interest in behavioral science, the last two decades have seen an explosion of new research and information—TED talks, books, workshops, apps—about practical tools that can help you change your behavior and encourage others to do the same.

But, as you've likely noticed, widely touted techniques don't always help you, or others, change. You forget to take your medication *again*, in spite of downloading that goal-setting app to help. You procrastinate on that big quarterly report for your boss in spite of setting daily reminders to work on it. Your employees don't take advantage of company-sponsored educational programs or retirement benefits even when they're offered rewards for signing up.

Why is it that these tools and techniques designed to spur change so often fail? One answer is that change is hard. But a more useful answer is that you haven't found the right strategy. Just as Andre Agassi spent years falling short of his potential by playing tennis with the wrong approach, we often fail by applying the wrong tactics in our attempts at change. Like Agassi, we search for solutions that will deliver the quick knockout victory and tend to ignore the specific nature of our adversary.

But to give yourself the best chance at success, it's critical to size up your opponent and develop a strategy tailored to overcome the particular challenges you face. The surest path to success is not one-size-fits-all. Instead, you must match your approach to your opponent.

In tennis, there's a generic playbook that works reasonably well: hit hard serves; run your opponent side to side; get to the net whenever you can. It's not a bad strategy. But if you're a really good tactician, like Gilbert, you'll take advantage of the fact that specific opponents have specific weaknesses. Maybe the player you're facing can't handle a low slice to the backhand side. You can torture them with that shot again and again and winning will be far easier.

Behavior change is similar. You can use an all-purpose strategy that works well on average. Set tough goals and break them down into component steps. Visualize success. Work to create habits—tiny ones, atomic ones, keystone ones—following the advice laid out in self-help bestsellers. But you'll get further faster if you customize your strategy: isolate the weakness preventing progress, and then pounce.

As an undergraduate and later as a PhD student in engineering, I was deeply bothered by the pesky human problems my friends and I couldn't seem to avoid. Why did I find it so hard to stop watching *Lost* and study for my tests? Why couldn't I get myself to go to the gym more regularly? Why did my roommates always put off homework until the last minute and eat Lucky Charms and Frosted Flakes for every meal? As an engineer who spent much of her time solving more technical problems, I was certain there must be a way to overcome these human struggles.

Then one day, during a required graduate course on microeconomics, I was introduced to behavioral economics—an entire field devoted to understanding, with analytical rigor and empirical depth, when and why people make flawed decisions. I was particularly taken with the idea of "nudging" people toward better choices, which was gaining popularity around the time I started my PhD. The founders of the "nudge movement," scholars Cass Sunstein and Richard Thaler, argued that because humans make predictably imperfect decisions, managers and policy makers can and should help them avoid common mistakes. The idea was that by nudging people toward objectively better choices (say, by putting healthy foods at eye level in the cafeteria or by simplifying the paperwork necessary to apply for government aid), you could improve their lives at little to no cost without restricting their freedom.

Suddenly, I realized it might be possible to develop nudges to tackle familiar problems, such as binge-watching *Lost* or failing to exercise. So I jumped on the nudge bandwagon, exploring how to nudge both myself and others into healthier choices and better financial decisions. Soon I was a gym regular and *Lost* marathons were in my rearview mirror.

But my interest in the power of nudging took on a new urgency a few years later when, as a newly minted assistant professor at Wharton, I was confronted with strong evidence that our small, daily failures to exercise or eat healthfully aren't trifling human foibles, but rather are serious matters of life and death. During an otherwise dull academic presentation, I encountered a pie chart that's been burned into my mind's eye ever since. The chart broke down why most Americans die earlier than they should. It turns out that the leading cause of premature death isn't poor health care, difficult social circumstances, bad genes, or environmental toxins. Instead, an estimated 40 percent of premature deaths are the result of personal behaviors we can change. I'm talking about daily, seemingly small decisions about eating, drinking, exercise, smoking, sex, and vehicle safety. These decisions add up, producing hundreds of thousands of fatal cancers, heart attacks, and accidents each year.

I was floored. I sat up a little straighter and thought, "Maybe I can do something about that forty percent."

And it was more than matters of life and death that grabbed my attention. While I've never seen a pie chart dissecting how our daily decisions affect our prosperity and our happiness, it stands to reason that our missteps accumulate in those areas of life, too.

Eager to make a difference, I shifted my focus and devoted nearly all of my waking hours to poring over research papers—old and new—exploring the science of behavior change. I talked with dozens of scholars from diverse disciplines about their most successful ideas, as well as their failed studies. And I worked with small start-ups as well as industry giants, such as Walmart and Google, to develop tools for nudging better decisions. As I tried to make sense of what worked well and what didn't, I began to see a consistent pattern. When policy makers, organizations, or scientists applied a one-size-fits-all strategy to change behavior, the results were mixed. But when they began by asking what stood in the way of progress—say, why their employees weren't saving enough money or getting flu shots—and *then* developed targeted strategies to change behavior, the results were far better.

I couldn't help but see the parallels to the way I'd been taught to think in engineering school. An engineer can't design a successful structure without first carefully accounting for the forces of opposition (say, wind resistance or gravity). So engineers always attempt to solve problems by first identifying the obstacles to success. Now, studying behavior change, I began to understand the power and promise of applying this same strategy. It's the very strategy that turned Andre Agassi's tennis career around by helping him refocus on his opponents' weaknesses.

Of course, when it comes to changing your behavior, your opponent isn't facing you across the net. Your opponent is inside your head. Maybe it's forgetfulness, or a lack of confidence, or laziness, or the tendency to succumb to temptation. Whatever the challenge, the best tacticians size up their opponent and play accordingly.

This book is intended to help you do exactly that. It takes Gilbert's winning strategy and applies it to behavior change. The chapters ahead show you how to identify your adversary, understand how that adversary tries to thwart your progress, and apply scientifically proven techniques that are tailor-made to vanquish it. Each chapter focuses on an internal obstacle that stands between you and success. By the time you're finished reading, you'll know how to recognize these obstacles and what can help you overcome them.

I've had the good fortune to collaborate with dozens of the world's best economists, psychologists, computer scientists, and doctors, all of whom share my goal of understanding how we can change behavior to improve lives. Our collective research has generated important insights that have already helped universities boost student achievement, medical practices cut down on unnecessary antibiotic prescriptions, nonprofits increase volunteering, and employers boost enrollment in benefits programs. We've also found techniques that can help anyone kick-start an exercise habit, improve their diet, increase the balance in their savings account, or get to the polls on Election Day.

By using these tools consistently, my hope is that you'll see small changes accumulate into big results. This is the approach that helped Andre Agassi turn his career around. He applied Brad Gilbert's philosophy one match at a time, using specifically tailored strategies to defeat each opponent in his path. And the wins added up. Soon after Agassi's surprise victory at the 1994 U.S. Open, he captured the number one world ranking, a title he would go on to hold for 101 weeks over the course of his now legendary career.

Brad Gilbert's advice made Agassi's transformation possible. And with the help of this book, my hope is that you, too, can turn the odds in your favor.

CHAPTER 1

Getting Started

When I first visited Google's sprawling corporate headquarters in 2012, I felt like a kid entering Willy Wonka's chocolate factory. The company's campus in Mountain View, California, boasts state-of-the-art everything, with a bit of whimsy on top. As I wound my way between office buildings, I encountered beach volleyball courts, fanciful sculptures, a gift shop stocked with branded tchotchkes, and free world-class restaurants. It was stunning.

Google had invited me and a group of other academics to its headquarters to attend a retreat for its senior human resources directors, but I couldn't help wondering what this company—one of the world's most innovative and successful—could possibly need from us. The smiling employees whizzing by on bikes painted in the primary colors of their company's logo certainly didn't look like they had any problems. Google had raked in 38 billion dollars in revenue the year before my visit.

But everyone has problems—even Google.

The company had convened the retreat to find new ways to help its employees make better decisions both at work and at home, with a particular emphasis on improving their productivity as well as their health and financial security (both of which have been linked to improved work performance). Midway through the event, Prasad Setty, a Wharton alum and Google vice president who had been in human resources for several years, asked me a seemingly innocuous question that would set me on the path to one of my most significant discoveries.

Google, he explained, offered its employees a wide range of benefits and programs designed to make their lives and jobs better and to solve such problems as undersaving for retirement, overuse of social media, physical inactivity, unhealthy eating, and smoking. But oddly enough, these programs weren't widely used. Prasad was both puzzled and frustrated that so many programs his team had created (which Google paid dearly for) went largely ignored. Why weren't employees clamoring to take advantage of free skill-building classes? Why weren't they all signing up for the company's 401(k) match and personal trainers?

Prasad had considered a few possible explanations, all of them plausible enough. Maybe the programs were being poorly advertised. Or maybe employees were just too busy to take advantage of them. But he also wondered about timing. Did I know, he asked, *when* Google should encourage employees to take advantage of these resources? Was there some ideal moment on the calendar or in someone's career to encourage behavior change?

I paused. Prasad's question was clearly important, and yet, to my knowledge, academics had largely overlooked it. If we hoped to effectively promote behavior change, of course we would need to understand *when* to begin.

Although I didn't have an easy answer for Prasad, I did have a hunch. I told him that before I could offer a reply grounded in solid evidence, I would need to review the academic literature and gather some data of my own. I started itching to get back to my research team in Philadelphia.

THE POWER OF A BLANK SLATE

Prasad was hardly the first leader I'd met who was perplexed by the stubborn persistence of unhealthy or unproductive behavior. I've spent countless hours talking with frustrated public health officials about how to reduce smoking, boost physical activity, improve diets, and increase vaccinations, and that's just for starters. I often hear the same exasperated plea: If you can't persuade people to alter their behavior by telling them that change is simple, cheap, and good for them, what magical ingredient will do the trick?

This book will offer many answers to that question (the most important being "It depends"), but one is particularly relevant to Prasad's problem. It starts with a remarkable medical success story.

Sudden infant death syndrome (SIDS) is every bit as terrifying as it sounds. Each year, tens of thousands of babies around the world die suddenly and inexplicably while sleeping. For years, SIDS has been a leading cause of death among infants in the United States between one month and one year of age. I remember being petrified when my pediatrician explained the risk factors during a checkup for my newborn son.

For decades, the medical establishment was at a loss over what to do about SIDS. But then, in the early 1990s, researchers made a major breakthrough. They discovered that infants put to sleep on their backs died of SIDS at half the rate of babies put to sleep on their stomachs. Half!

This was a discovery worthy of celebration—and fast action. It presented an opportunity to save hundreds of thousands of lives, so naturally, the public health community wasted no time spreading the word. The U.S. government launched an ambitious Back to Sleep campaign to educate new parents about the importance of placing babies to sleep on their backs. The National Institutes of Health flooded the airwaves with commercials and filled hospitals and doctors' offices with brochures.

Of course, there was no guarantee of success. Many such campaigns fail, which explains my frequent phone calls with frustrated public health officials. Just consider the recent high-profile attempt to reduce obesity by requiring calorie labeling in chain restaurants. It turns out that telling people how many calories are in a Big Mac or a Frappuccino reduces calorie consumption, well . . . essentially not at all. Or consider the efforts by U.S. health authorities, starting in 2010, to persuade Americans to get annual flu shots. The effects have been minimal at best: 43 percent of Americans now get flu shots, up from 39 percent before the policy was implemented. So there was every reason to expect that the Back to Sleep campaign would be the same old story, making only a small dent in a massive problem.

Thankfully, the campaign worked wonders. Between 1993 and 2010, the percentage of infants put to sleep on their backs in the United States shot up, more than quadrupling from 17 percent to 73 percent, and deaths from SIDS plummeted. The message hasn't gone out of style. In 2016, decades after the campaign began, my doctor handed me a Back to Sleep pamphlet when I gave birth in Philadelphia.

But if Back to Sleep was unquestionably a huge success, why had so many other, similar campaigns floundered? Prasad's question about timing inspired me to formulate a hypothesis.

The moment you become a parent is unquestionably one of life's starkest turning points. Just a day before your child's arrival, there was no helpless baby to feed, clothe, protect, and soothe; then boom—all of that changes. Everything about parenthood is new and different, and as a result, you have no old habits to break, no long-standing routines to disrupt. You're truly starting fresh, for better and worse. The message of Back to Sleep arrives at this critical juncture, when you're not yet set in your ways and are motivated to try to do everything right. My hunch was that the timing couldn't be better for changing patterns in people's behavior. No matter what your parents did or their parents before that, when a doctor tells you that it's vital to put your baby to sleep on their back, you're eager to comply and don't have to fight against bad habits.

Compare this with a public health campaign that attempts to influence eating, smoking, or vaccination habits for adults. These kinds of initiatives catch us in the middle of our busy lives, with entrenched routines that limit our openness to change. Even though the information can make the difference between life and death, it's no wonder that we often ignore it.

After my visit to Google, I came to suspect that this was an incredibly important but underappreciated insight: if you want to change your behavior or someone else's, you're at a huge advantage if you begin with a blank slate—a fresh start—and no old habits working against you.

There's just one problem: true blank slates are incredibly rare. Almost all of the behaviors we want to change are everyday, customary, and baked into our hectic and well-established routines.

But thankfully, change in the absence of a blank slate isn't hopeless—it's just hard. The hunch I had at Google was that there might be a way to harness the *feeling* of a blank slate, even in moments when no true tabula rasa exists.

THE FRESH START EFFECT

As soon as I got back from my visit to Google in 2012, I set up a meeting with my doctoral student Hengchen Dai (now a professor at UCLA) and Jason Riis, a visiting faculty member from Harvard. I was eager to tell them about Prasad's question and my intuition that people might be more open to change when they feel they have a fresh start.

As I explained my thinking, Hengchen and Jason lit up. Like me, they immediately grasped that timing could be critically important to change. We knew that people instinctively gravitate toward moments that feel like fresh starts when they want to make change happen. Just think of New Year's resolutions. And yet economic theory has always posited that our preferences remain stable over time unless we face changing circumstances, such as new constraints, new information, or a price shock that forces an adjustment to our beliefs or budget. Hengchen, Jason, and I suspected this assumption was incorrect and that there were, in fact, systematic and predictable moments when our circumstances don't change but we still feel compelled to change ourselves. In our excitement, we began sharing stories of times when fresh starts had prompted us to behave differently, discussing what each example had in common, and searching for insights about why our motivation had shifted.

Most of the changes we'd initiated around fresh starts had been small—working to kick a nail-biting habit, getting back behind the steering wheel after a driving scare, or exploring new dating strategies after a romantic slump. But I'd heard stories about more momentous changes, too. Take Scott Harrison, author of the bestselling book *Thirst*, for example. Scott famously took inspiration from New Year's Day to abandon his profession as a hard-partying club promoter for a life of sobriety and nonprofit work. Fresh starts seemed capable of inspiring substantial change.

During our team huddle, Hengchen, Jason, and I were particularly quick to acknowledge the power of the New Year, but we had an inkling that this was just one well-known example of a broader phenomenon—one of many moments when people feel especially ready to change because they have the sense that they've been given a fresh start. The challenge would be to identify other moments that provoke the same reaction and to understand how and why they can unstick us and motivate change.

To get started, Hengchen began digging into existing research on how people think about special dates such as New Year's, and she came back with an intriguing discovery. Her search led her to a literature in psychology on how people think about the passage of time. She learned that rather than perceiving time as a continuum, we tend to think about our lives in "episodes," creating story arcs from the notable incidents, or chapters, in our lives. One chapter might start the day you move into your college dorm ("the college years"), another with your first job ("the consulting era"), another on your fortieth birthday, and yet another at the start of a new year or millennium.

This research helped us develop the idea that the start of a new life chapter, no matter how small, might be able to give people the impression of a clean slate. These new chapters are moments when the labels we use to describe ourselves, who we are, and what we're living through shift, compelling us to shift with them. We go from "student" to "working professional"; "renter" to "homeowner"; "single" to "married"; "adult" to "parent"; "New Yorker" to "Californian"; "denizen of the 90s" to "twenty-first-century American" all in the flip of a switch. And labels matter to our behavior. When we're labeled "voters" (instead of people who vote), "carrot eaters" (instead of people who eat carrots whenever they can), and "Shakespeare readers" (instead of people who read Shakespeare a lot), it influences how we *act*, not just how we describe ourselves.

If you've ever made a New Year's resolution, confidently predicting that the "new you" in the "new year" would be able to make a change, the potency of labels may resonate. Probably my favorite story about the power of New Year's comes from Ray Zahab, who was a guest on a podcast I host about decision making. Ray used the arrival of a new millennium, which ended the 1990s chapter of his life and began a new chapter, to turn his life around.

Before he managed to transform his life, Ray was a heavy smoker and drinker who would sometimes eat McDonald's for every meal. But when he reached his early thirties, Ray was desperate to make a change. He was tired of being broke and out of shape.

He wondered if he could be more like his brother, a successful long-distance runner, but he knew long-distance running was out of the question for a smoker. The obvious first step would be to quit.

But he just couldn't. He tried and tried, but the cravings always pulled him back. He needed something more to push him over the edge.

And then Ray had an idea. He would use the turn of the century— New Year's Eve, 1999—to quit for good. "I used that date because it had such a huge finality, it seemed, in everyone's minds," Ray explained. "I mean, it was the end of the century, right? This was a reset switch for humanity."

Shortly before midnight on December 31, Ray smoked his last cigarette. "If I can't do it now, then I'll never be able to do it," he told himself.

The next morning, Ray woke up with a strong craving for a cigarette. "But it was January 1, 2000," he recalled, and with the arrival of the new millennium, he had crossed an important threshold—he was no longer the same Ray who had been unable to kick his nicotine habit. "Something in me, a little spark, said 'I can do this.'"

And Ray did do it—he quit for good.

In 2003, he won the 100-mile Yukon Arctic Ultra, one of the world's most extreme endurance races. He's quick to note that his victory started on the first day of 2000. That moment made everything else possible.

Ray is a dramatic example of someone who took inspiration from the start of a new year to make a life change. But every January 1, about 40 percent of Americans resolve to make life improvements: to get fit, save more for retirement, quit drinking, or learn a foreign language.

With the shift to a new year, it's almost as if past attempts to stay off social media, earn As in school, be a better colleague, and eat healthier can be dismissed as the failures of another person. Last year you couldn't cut it at work or failed to quit smoking, but "that was the old me," you think, "and this is the new me."

Hengchen, Jason, and I suspected that if people really felt that they were new and improved, it could, in some cases, be enough to help them overcome a meaningful obstacle to change. But we needed to put our idea to the test.

To start, we gathered information about when people naturally pursue change. Across data set after data set, we found the same patterns. Undergraduates at a campus fitness center were more likely to visit the gym not only in January, but also earlier in the week, after a school holiday, at the beginning of a new semester, and after their birthdays. (Unless it was a twenty-first birthday—can you guess why?) Similarly, in January, on Mondays, and after holiday breaks, we documented an uptick in online goal setting (tracked by stickK, a popular goal-setting website) and in "diet" searches on Google. We also found that people's birthdays were linked with more goal creation on stickK.

Our analyses produced a remarkably consistent picture of what Hengchen, Jason, and I have come to call the "fresh start effect."

When we surveyed a panel of Americans about how they feel on fresh start dates such as New Year's or their birthday, we heard again and again that new beginnings offer a kind of psychological "do-over." People feel distanced from their past failures; they feel like a different person—a person with reason to be optimistic about the future.

We're more likely to pursue change on dates that feel like new beginnings because these moments help us overcome a common obstacle to goal initiation: the sense that we've failed before and will, thus, fail again.

This explains why every Monday, I'm sure the week ahead will be more productive than the last, and why so many of my friends set resolutions not just at New Year's but on their birthdays, too. These new beginnings can also lead us to pause, reflect, and think about the bigger picture, which makes us more likely to consider trying to make a change.

Now that Hengchen, Jason, and I had this evidence in hand and a solid understanding of why fresh starts seem to matter, we couldn't help but wonder if there were other moments charged with life-altering potential.

BEYOND THE CALENDAR

In the early 1970s, Bob Pass, a trial attorney in the U.S. government's Federal Power Commission, stopped by the great ape exhibit during a visit to the National Zoo with his girlfriend. Looking at the caged gorillas, he turned to her and lamented, "I know exactly how they feel."

Soon after, Bob took a hiatus from his legal career to clear his head, travel, and give tennis lessons at a local country club. He found that he was happier than he'd ever been when working as a lawyer, but he knew it couldn't last—he wanted a wife and kids, and he thought that supporting a family would require a steady job like the one he'd left behind.

Soon enough, he found himself back in a suit, interviewing for an opening at a local law firm. Everything was going swimmingly until he started to feel so ill that he had to be driven home. Within two days, he was in the hospital with a staph infection in a heart valve, unsure if he would recover.

In the end, the experience would prove pivotal. While lying in bed worrying about life and death, Bob thought hard about his past and present, including the job offer he'd just received. His conclusion was crystal clear: he hated being a lawyer. His brush with mortality served as a chance to envision a new path. In his words, "It forced me to confront my life."

Bob realized that he loved coaching tennis. He declined the steady job as an attorney and started a tennis academy in 1973 with just a handful of students. Decades later, when I was a student at his thriving academy, he shared his story with me and told me it was the best decision of his life.*

Once I began thinking, night and day, about fresh starts, I could see that Bob's health scare bookended one chapter of his life and gave him the courage to start a new chapter. But the calendar had nothing to do with it; Bob owed his fresh start to a meaningful life event.

For my former tennis coach, illness provided the impetus to start over. But research suggests it could just as easily have been a cross-country move, a promotion at work, or perhaps even something as mundane as a disruption to his commute.

In a paper published in 1994, two psychologists surveyed more than a hundred people who had sought to make a meaningful life change, such as switching careers, ending a personal relationship, or starting a diet. Remarkably, they found that 36 percent of successful attempts took place when people moved homes, whereas only 13 percent of unsuccessful attempts followed a move. These statistics sug-

---

*If you're noticing a tennis theme in my stories, never fear—tennis will not dominate these pages. But I should acknowledge that competing seriously in the sport as a young adult taught me many lessons that have informed my thinking and research on behavior change.

gest that when we're seeking to change, the disruptions to our lives triggered by physical transitions can be just as powerful as the fresh starts spurred by new beginnings on our calendars.

Yet, unlike calendar dates, these fresh starts *don't* contradict the predictions of economic theory, because they actually *change* our life circumstances—they don't just shift our perspective. And in doing so, they can help us discover new paths to change we'd never noticed. Consider the London Underground strike in February of 2014, which caused the closures of some London tube stations and forced hundreds of thousands of commuters to experiment with new travel routes. This disruption introduced some people to new and more efficient itineraries, producing positive, lasting changes to the commuting habits of roughly 5 percent of Underground riders. Physical disruptions, such as a move or a transit strike, can unsettle old behaviors and help us recognize a better approach. But they also come with the same benefits that accompany purely *psychological* fresh starts, opening new chapters in our autobiographical memories, which can make change feel more manageable and attractive.

Notably, though, all disruptions aren't created equal. Take a study of Texas A&M transfer students, some of whom had come from out of town and some of whom had transferred from a local junior college. The study compared those whose environments stayed the same with those whose environments shifted. Some transfer students experienced only minor changes in their environments—maintaining most of their routines and interacting with the same friends in the same haunts, while others experienced more substantive disruptions.

The study explored whether the kind of change a student experienced might alter their TV watching, newspaper reading, and exercise habits. And in fact, the magnitude of the shift mattered quite a bit. The students (many from the local junior college) whose environments hadn't changed substantially mostly kept to their old routines, while their peers who had made a bigger transition were more likely to change their behavior. Likewise, in our research, Hengchen, Jason, and I had seen that some calendar dates seem to provoke larger reactions than others. New Year's, for instance, typically exerts a far greater influence on behavior than, say, your typical Monday. The bigger the landmark, the more likely it is to help us take a step back, regroup, and make a clean break from the past.

The more I've thought about this research, the clearer it's become to me that the potential to harness fresh starts is underutilized. When we hope to change, we have an opportunity to try reshaping our environment to help us disrupt old routines and ways of thinking. This could be as simple as finding a new coffee shop to work in or a new gym. And we should be looking for opportunities to capitalize on other life changes, too, to reevaluate what matters most to us. Whether it's an illness, a promotion, or a move to another town, it could offer just the disruption needed to turn your life around.

THE DOWNSIDE OF FRESH STARTS

Two years after my trip to Google, my PhD student Hengchen came to me with an idea for her doctoral dissertation. She wanted to study Major League Baseball (MLB), which surprised me because she'd never struck me as a sports fan.

But her newfound fascination with the MLB made sense when she explained a curious feature of the rules that guide player trades between the National and American Leagues. Did I know, she asked, that when players are traded midseason across leagues, their statistics for the season are calculated anew, as if their season were just starting? But for within-league trades, statistics for the season continue to be tallied as if nothing had changed.

Suddenly, I understood. Hengchen was excited about baseball because the "resets" associated with cross-league trades represent a kind of fresh start for the players—a literal clean slate for their statistics. In all of the research we'd done together on fresh starts, we hadn't yet focused on such resets.

But resets are all around us. Each day when I wake up, my Fitbit tells me I've taken zero steps so far—my total from the previous day is history and I get to start anew. Likewise, each semester, when students walk into my classroom for the first time, all the work they've done in previous courses has no impact on the grade they'll earn from me. Wherever you look, earnings reports, sales records, and other statistical compilations of performance are constantly being wiped clean, yearly, monthly, weekly. And yet when Hengchen approached me with her dissertation idea, we knew very little about how these resets affected people's progress toward their goals.

In order to change that, Hengchen wanted to explore what happens when two statistically indistinguishable baseball players experience a major change—a trade to a new team—but only one is offered a clean slate. Imagine two players, Jackie Robinson and Jackie Robins, who've performed equally well at bat in the season-to-date. Now imagine that both get traded to new teams, but Jackie Robinson is traded across leagues, so his season-to-date statistics are reset, while Jackie Robins gets to hold on to his season-to-date statistics when he's traded within-league. What would happen next?

When Hengchen analyzed forty years of MLB data, she found the answer depends on how the Jackies have been performing so far. First, she determined that players who were performing badly* got a leg up when they switched leagues. Consistent with our past work on fresh starts, Hengchen found that these players saw greater improvement in the period post-trade than those who were traded within-league.

When I was a graduate student in 2004, my hometown team (the Boston Red Sox) benefited from just such a midseason reset when the shortstop Orlando Cabrera came over from the Montreal Expos in a cross-league trade. Early in the season, Orlando was batting just .246, which was well below the MLB average of .265 that year. But when he moved to the Red Sox, his season-to-date statistics were reset, and his batting average spiked 29 percent to .294, much to the delight of Boston's baseball fans.

More strikingly, Hengchen also found evidence that fresh starts aren't always positive. Across the board, players who'd had high batting averages† before a trade (suggesting that they were really on a roll that season) tended to see their performance *drop* afterward. And notably, the drop was much larger when a player's batting average was wiped clean by a cross-league trade (proving that this pattern wasn't just regression to the mean). Instead of getting a performance boost from a trade as struggling players had, top performers *suffered* from resets, which made their recent successes feel farther in the rearview mirror and forced them to rebuild their record from scratch.

Jarrod Saltalamacchia learned the hard way that fresh starts can be a downer when everything has been going your way. A catcher

---

*Poor performance was defined as a batting average of at least one standard deviation below the mean in the league in a given year in Hengchen's research.

†Defined as one standard deviation above mean in the league in a given year in Hengchen's research.

who was batting a solid .284 with the Atlanta Braves in 2007, Salta-lamacchia was traded midseason across leagues to the Texas Rangers. And just as Hengchen would have expected, by October, his batting average had dropped 13 percent to .251.

The baseball study was one of several Hengchen ran showing the same pattern. In experiments where she hired people to do tasks such as word searches or track their personal goals, Hengchen found again and again that resets helped underperformers up their game but harmed people who were already doing well.

This was an important and cautionary lesson: Not everyone benefits from a fresh start. When you're on a roll, any disruption can be a setback. We see this at home and at work, and though the disruption itself might seem like no big deal, even trivial, the consequences can weigh you down. Think about how it feels to be in the flow at work, only to be interrupted by an unwanted call or a chatty co-worker. That one intrusion can be enough to throw you off for the rest of the day. Or maybe you were making great progress with a new health regimen—smoothies for breakfast, salads for lunch, home-cooked dinners every night. But then came your summer vacation, and countless funnel cakes later, you never did get back to your healthy habits.

Hengchen's finding gave me a new perspective on some older studies. In two projects where researchers attempted to help college undergraduates develop new gym-going habits (one of which I conducted), the same nasty pattern had reared its head. In both studies, holiday breaks turned out to be negative influences: students who had formed new gym habits failed to resume them after they returned to campus. The effect of the disruptions was total, reversing the students' progress.

These findings, combined with Hengchen's, make it clear that while fresh starts are helpful for kick-starting change, they can also be unwelcome disruptors of well-functioning routines. Anyone seeking to *maintain* good habits should beware.

WHEN TO ENCOURAGE CHANGE

One day in the fall of 2014, thousands of people around the United States opened their mailboxes to find a letter. In large white print against a red background, each mailing boldly proclaimed, "Stop Waiting . . . Start Saving!"

Everyone who got this message had two things in common: they worked for one of several large universities partnering with me and a team of collaborators on a research study; and they were not yet saving much, if at all, for retirement.

Past research has shown that many nonsavers really do *want* to set aside a portion of each paycheck for the future. They just haven't gotten around to it. So Hengchen and I teamed up with two experts in savings, John Beshears and Shlomo Benartzi, to find a way to make saving really easy—our letters doubled as forms people could send back in a preaddressed, stamped envelope. All it took was a signature and a check mark in the right box for people who got our mailings to start saving more. We'd then take care of the rest, ensuring a small chunk of future paychecks would be diverted to a retirement savings account.

While we were excited to help more people save money, what was most interesting to my team was to find out if it would matter *when* we invited people to start making their deductions. We offered everyone the opportunity to start saving right away, but we assumed many people would prefer to postpone the pain of getting a smaller paycheck at least a bit. And we had an inkling that we could convince more people to start saving simply by inviting the change at the right time. Which brings me back to the question about timing that Prasad Setty asked me when I visited Google.

So far, everything I've told you about fresh starts supports my suspicion that they were the answer to Prasad's question. But the research I've described proves only that fresh starts are moments when people *naturally* undertake change. It actually leaves Prasad's question unanswered: he wanted to know when Google should *facilitate* change.

Some survey experiments I did with Hengchen and Jason did hint at an answer to his specific question. In several studies, we recruited undergraduates at the University of Pennsylvania who had goals they'd been meaning to pursue, and we promised to help them get started. Then we invited these students to sign up for email reminders to kick off new and improved behaviors on a specific future date. The experimental twist was that we varied how we characterized the future dates. In one study, we described March 20 as "the first day of spring" for some students and "the third Thursday in March" for others. In another study, we described May 14 as "the first day of Penn's summer break" for some students and "Penn's administrative day" (a meaningless designation we invented) for others.

Confirming our suspicion about the usefulness of fresh start dates, in both of these studies (and others), when we suggested that a date was associated with a new beginning (such as "the first day of spring"), students viewed it as a more attractive time to kick-start goal pursuit than when we presented it as an unremarkable day (such as "the third Thursday in March"). Whether it was starting a new gym habit, improving sleep hygiene, or spending less time on social media, when the date we suggested was associated with a new beginning, more students wanted to receive our reminders to change right then. Follow-up research by other behavioral scientists showed a similar pattern among prospective dieters.* And more recent research by a different team found that similar benefits were achieved by showing goal seekers modified weekly calendars. When calendars depicted the current day (either Monday or Sunday) as the first day of the week, people reported feeling more motivated to make immediate progress on their goals.

But these results all came from small survey studies, some of which merely asked people to predict what they would do instead of actually tracking their behavior. In addition, many were run with undergraduates, who don't necessarily make decisions like the rest of us. I wanted to know if the intention to change actually resulted in action. That's why my collaborators and I sent our letters with bright red proclamations to thousands of university employees, urging them to save for retirement—we wanted to see if fresh starts could help older adults with more entrenched routines make meaningful changes in their lives.

Retirement planning matters immensely to long-term well-being, but most Americans save far too little. If fresh starts could influence

---

*Two psychologists ran experiments that altered the kinds of calendars would-be dieters viewed when planning ahead. Some calendars showed only days of the week, such as Sunday, Monday, and Tuesday, while others labeled only days of the month, such as February 28, March 1, and March 2. The researchers found that prospective dieters reported a higher likelihood of starting their improved eating regimens on the first day of a new month when viewing a calendar featuring days of the month. When presented with a calendar featuring days of the week, however, Mondays instead became a highly attractive start date.

momentous decisions about how much people set aside in their retirement accounts, we'd know we were onto something. So, in addition to the option to start saving immediately, we offered some people the chance to start saving at a later date. For some it was a fresh start date—after their next birthday or at the start of spring. Others were not pointed to a fresh start date but rather to an arbitrary, unlabeled future date or an upcoming holiday without fresh start connotations, such as Martin Luther King Jr. Day.

The power of the labeled fresh start was impressive. The post-cards that encouraged employees to begin saving after their next birthday or at the start of spring were 20 to 30 percent more effective than the "ordinary" mailings that allowed people to begin saving at a more arbitrary future date. By reminding people of an upcoming fresh start, we were able to make the same opportunity for behavior change more appealing. These findings show that it may be possible to boost a wide range of goal-directed behaviors if we just get the timing of our invitations right—from enrolling in online classes to purchasing energy-efficient appliances to scheduling health checkups.

With so much convergent evidence, I feel much more confident today making predictions about the best time to encourage behavior change than I did during my trip to Google in 2012, and at least some people are listening. After I shared my fresh start research with Prasad, Google programmers built a "moments engine" that identifies when the company's employees are likely to be open to change (say, after a promotion or a move to a new office). The moments engine then sends employees nudges to spur action at these points in time.

Happily, Google is not alone in thinking more strategically about when to encourage behavior change. From nonprofits timing their fundraising campaigns to HR consultancies scheduling their nudges, more and more organizations are using fresh starts to help people kick-start change.

LOOK FOR FRESH START OPPORTUNITIES

Since publishing my research with Hengchen and Jason on the fresh start effect, each year around New Year's Day my inbox is flooded with emails from reporters, TV anchors, radio personalities, and podcasters who want to tap my expertise on this topic.

But once we've talked for a bit about the power of fresh starts, many journalists bring up a well-known and dispiriting statistic from a 2007 survey: One third of Americans' New Year's resolutions bomb by the end of January, and four fifths fail overall. As a result, nearly every interviewer asks me the same cynical but fair question: If so many resolutions fail, why bother? Shouldn't we just cancel this silly tradition?

Of course, I understand where they're coming from. I've been frustrated with failed resolutions in the past, too, and I'm committed to teaching more people about the science that can help them succeed. But this question still drives me a little crazy. As actor David Hasselhoff has said, "If you're not in the game, you can't hit a home run."

In my opinion, New Year's resolutions are great! So are spring resolutions, birthday resolutions, and Monday resolutions. Any time you make a resolution, you're putting yourself in the game. Too often, a sense that change is difficult and daunting prevents us from taking the leap to try. Maybe you like the idea of making a change, but actually doing it seems hard, and so you feel unmotivated to start. Maybe you've failed when you attempted to change before and expect to fail again. Often, change takes multiple attempts to stick.

I like to remind cynics that if you flip the discouraging statistics about New Year's resolutions on their head, you'll see that 20 percent of the goals set each January *succeed*. That's a lot of people who've changed their lives for the better simply because they resolved to try in the first place. Just think of Ray Zahab, transforming himself from an unhappy, out-of-shape smoker to a world-class athlete. For some people, fresh starts can help prompt small changes. But they can also inspire transformative change by giving you the *will* to try pursuing a daunting goal.

So, if you're hoping to make a positive change in your life but are pessimistic about your chances, perhaps because you've failed before and worry another attempt is likely to turn out similarly, my advice is to look for fresh start opportunities. Is there an upcoming date that could represent a clean break with the past? It could be a birthday, the start of summer, or even just a Monday. Can you change your physical circumstances (or help your employees change theirs)? Moving to a new home or office might be impractical, but working at a café or changing some of your other routines could be enough to make a difference. Or is there anything you can do to reset the way you're tracking success? OK, so you don't coach a professional baseball team, but maybe you could break your yearly sales goals into monthly ones to give yourself (or your employees who are struggling) more frequent resets. Just be careful not to disrupt routines when they're working well.

Once you've found or created the right moment to start, the next question is how to succeed on the journey to change.

———— Chapter Takeaways ————

- An ideal time to consider pursuing change is after a fresh start.

- Fresh starts increase your motivation to change because they give you either a real clean slate or the impression of one; they relegate your failures more cleanly to the past; and they boost your optimism about the future. They can also disrupt bad habits and lead you to think bigger picture about your life.

- Fresh starts can be calendar dates that mark new beginnings (a new year, season, month, or week), birthdays, or anniversaries. They can also be triggered by meaningful life events, such as a health scare or a move to a new town. And finally, resets—when the metrics you're using to track your performance are set back to zero—can also offer fresh starts.

- Although fresh starts can jolt you into positive change, they can also interrupt you when you're on a roll, reversing your progress, so beware.

- A particularly effective time to encourage *other* people— employees, friends, or family members—to pursue positive change is after fresh starts.

CHAPTER 2

Impulsivity

S tockholm's Odenplan metro station is a bustling transit hub in the heart of Sweden's capital city and busiest urban center. Each day, nearly a hundred thousand passengers rush through the station heading to and from work, home, doctors' appointments, shopping trips, business meetings, dinners with friends, and wherever else they need to go.

Entering and exiting the Odenplan station was always a pretty ordinary experience—you used the stairs or the escalator—until one night in 2009 when a team of technicians funded by Volkswagen set to work on something unusual. As Stockholm slept, they began laying down large black-and-white panels across the stairs leading up from the metro station into the city. And just in time for the sunrise, the technicians put the finishing touches on their masterpiece.

What they'd crafted was something of a technical and artistic marvel. The normally drab staircase leading passengers from the subterranean Odenplan station to the street was transformed into a set of giant, working piano keys.

Video taken of the exit before the installation shows almost every pedestrian ignoring the stairs in favor of the escalator. But on the day the piano stairs appeared, people of all ages did a double take as they encountered an unexpected pleasure in their paths.

When I show a film about this engineering marvel during presentations I give at companies around the world, we all smile while watching adults, toddlers, and even dogs hopping up and down to make music as they exit the busy subway station. People compose duets, take videos, hold hands, and laugh uproariously as they interact with a strange new plaything. Astoundingly, the film reports that 66 percent more Odenplan metro visitors chose the stairs over the escalator after the piano keys appeared, which is exactly what the Volkswagen team hoped would happen. Knowing that walking up even a few extra steps each day can make a difference to people's health, they designed the piano stairs as a creative solution to a common problem.*

The reason I share this entertaining video with corporate audiences is not to suggest that we all install musical staircases in our homes and offices, but to vividly illustrate what I view as one of the biggest barriers to behavior change and an often-overlooked way of surmounting it.

The barrier is simple: Doing the "right" thing is often unsatisfying in the short-term. You know you should take the stairs, but you're tired, and the escalator beckons. You know you should focus on important tasks at work but scrolling through social media is more fun.

---

*A staggering 9 percent of premature deaths worldwide are attributable to inadequate exercise (I-Min Lee et al., "Effect of Physical Inactivity on Major Non-Communicable Diseases Worldwide: An Analysis of Burden of Disease and Life Expectancy," *The Lancet* 380, no. 9838 [2012]: 219–29, DOI:10.1016/S0140-6736(12)61031-9).

You mean to keep your temper in check but yelling at an irritating colleague is more satisfying. And you know you ought to keep your nose in your books the night before a big test but binge-watching your favorite Shonda Rhimes show is far more enticing. Economists call this tendency to favor instantly gratifying temptations over larger long-term rewards "present bias," though its common name is "impulsivity," and it's unfortunately universal.

Naturally, it's a challenge I've personally faced. My most pernicious duel with present bias arose when I was an engineering graduate student in Boston. I found that if I didn't make the time to exercise, I often melted down as I tried to write code and prepare for tests late into the night. But even though I knew exercise was important for both my physical and mental health, after a long day of classes, the idea of changing into sweats and tromping off to the gym was repellent, particularly in the dead of Boston's brutal winters.

"How in the world can I get myself to go to the gym?" I would whine to my then fiancé, now husband. One day, exasperated, he made an excellent (if obvious) point: "You're an engineer. Can't you engineer a solution?"

Oddly, although my mind at that point was consumed with engineering problems, I hadn't been thinking about *this* problem in those terms. My fiancé's snarky comment prompted me to put on my engineering hat and consider the forces working against me so I could find a way to repel them. In this case, the forces of opposition were simple. The thing I knew I *should* do—hit the gym after a long day of classes—wasn't instantly gratifying. To solve my problem, I realized I would need to figure out how to *make it* instantly gratifying.

JUST A SPOONFUL OF SUGAR

The Disney classic *Mary Poppins*, featuring Julie Andrews as the world's most marvelous nanny, came out in 1964 to widespread critical acclaim and popular delight. As you probably know, Mary Poppins is tasked with taking care of two adorable but incorrigible British children whose parents tend to neglect their needs. Where other nannies failed miserably at keeping these mischievous charges in line, Poppins succeeds with outlandish antics and memorable songs.

What you likely don't know is that Julie Andrews initially refused the title role in *Mary Poppins* because she didn't like one of the songs her character was meant to sing. In an effort to get her on board, Walt Disney tasked the renowned lyricists Bob and Richard Sherman with quickly composing something catchier.

As Bob frantically searched for a new and better idea, fate happily intervened. His eight-year-old son came home from school one day and reported that he'd just had his polio vaccine. Imagining it had been a painful shot, Bob asked if it had hurt. And his son's reply provided much-needed inspiration for what is now one of the most popular children's songs of all time: "Oh no; they just put a drop of medicine on a lump of sugar."

Oddly enough, research has shown that we rarely follow this wise approach and sweeten the deal when we set out to pursue our long-term goals. Instead, we tend to pursue behavior change without thinking of the discomfort we'll have to endure or attempting to alleviate it. When committing to a healthy new eating regimen, we buy a basket of the most sinless foods—broccoli, carrots, kale, and quinoa—without regard for taste. When starting a nighttime degree, we register first for the most useful class we can find, even if it's likely to be a bear. When joining a new gym, we head straight for the punishing but maximally efficient StairMaster.

In fact, in one study of the way people tackle change, more than two thirds of respondents told researchers that they typically focus on the benefits they expect to accrue in the *long-run* without regard for their short-term pain. Only 26 percent of those surveyed said they would try to make goal pursuit enjoyable in and of itself.

There's a good explanation for this: those long-term benefits are typically the impetus for pursuing a goal or making a change. If it weren't for the long-term benefits of exercise, studying, saving, healthy eating, and so on, many of us would never bother.

But there's reason to worry that an eyes-on-the-prize mentality could be a mistake. Lots of research shows that we tend to be over-confident about how easy it is to be self-disciplined. This is why so many of us optimistically buy expensive gym memberships when paying per-visit fees would be cheaper, register for online classes we'll never complete, and purchase family-size chips on discount to trim our monthly snack budget, only to consume every last crumb in a single sitting. We think "future me" will be able to make good choices, but too often "present me" succumbs to temptation.

People have a remarkable ability to ignore their own failures. Even when we flounder again and again, many of us manage to maintain a rosy optimism about our ability to do better next time rather than learning from our past mistakes. We latch on to fresh starts and other reasons to stay upbeat, which may help us get out of bed in the morning but can prevent us from approaching change in the smartest possible way.

Don't get me wrong. Fresh starts are great for helping us take the initiative to *begin* pursuing a tough goal. But they can prevent us from pursuing it wisely if we don't take into account other obstacles, such as present bias. If the thought of going running at 5:00 A.M. makes you want to gag in October, it will probably still be unappealing when you ring in the New Year.

Recognizing this, the psychologists Ayelet Fishbach and Kaitlin Woolley suspected that people could tackle tough goals more effectively if they stopped overestimating their willpower. They predicted that if people focused on making long-term goal pursuit more enjoyable in the *short-term* by adding the proverbial lump of sugar to their medicine, they'd be far more successful.

In one study, Ayelet and Kaitlin encouraged participants to eat more healthy foods. In another, they encouraged more exercise. The twist was that some study participants (chosen at random) were prompted to select the kinds of healthy foods or exercises they expected to *enjoy* most while others were simply encouraged to pick the ones they'd *benefit* from most (which is what the majority of us do naturally).

Ayelet and Kaitlin discovered that encouraging people to find the fun in healthy activities led to substantially better results, leading people to persist longer in their workouts and eat more healthy food. Their discovery looks suspiciously like what happened in Stockholm's Odenplan subway station. But it's worth remembering that these results, while intuitive to some degree, fly squarely in the face of the way the vast majority of us report approaching our goals—with too much faith in our self-control and ability to do tough things.

Rather than believing we'll be able to "just do it" (as Nike implores us), we can make more progress if we recognize that we struggle to do what's distasteful in the moment and look for ways to make those activities sweeter.

Mary Poppins's memorable refrain "a spoonful of sugar makes the medicine go down" follows another line in the song that even more perfectly encapsulates the idea behind Ayelet and Kaitlin's research: "In every job that must be done, there is an element of fun. You find the fun, and snap! The job's a game." The song works in part because the wisdom rings so true. Anyone who has taken care of children knows it's absurd to tell them to focus on the long-term benefits of completing a chore. If it isn't fun, kids simply won't do it.

Although adults have somewhat better neural circuitry for delaying gratification than children, we're fundamentally wired the same way. We just fail to recognize it.

Unfortunately, when I was a graduate student struggling to exercise, Ayelet and Kaitlin hadn't yet done their seminal work, so I didn't have their insights to build on. But my fiancé's suggestion that I engineer a solution to my problems gave me a similar idea—one that would eventually help me combat a wide range of self-control dilemmas (not just my own), and which unintentionally used both Mary Poppins's wisdom and Ayelet and Kaitlin's discovery (before they had even discovered it).

TEMPTATION BUNDLING

When I was a first-year graduate student struggling to get myself to the gym, I was also facing another challenge. Instead of turning to my problem sets and assigned readings each afternoon following a grueling day of classes, I tended to procrastinate and curl up on my couch with a juicy page-turner. I particularly loved potboilers by authors such as James Patterson and J. K. Rowling. For me, novels were the ultimate indulgence.

But obviously, reading fiction was not the best use of my time. I was trying to earn a PhD in engineering—I needed to buckle down and study. The message came in loud and clear during midterms my second semester in Boston when I checked my grade in one of my toughest computer science classes and discovered I was on track to fail. I'd never failed a class before or even come close. Something had to change.

Thankfully, my fiancé's challenge led to an epiphany about how I could simultaneously boost my exercise and stop procrastinating on schoolwork. What if I let myself indulge in reading the page-turners I craved only while working out, I wondered? If I could swing it, I realized I'd stop wasting time at home reading *Harry Potter* when I should be studying, *and* I'd start craving trips to the gym to find out what would happen next in my latest novel. Not only that, but I'd enjoy my novel and my workout more combined—I wouldn't feel guilty reading the novel, and time would fly by at the gym.

Considering the idea further, I realized a similar technique might allow me to solve lots of other self-control problems I faced. I started to see opportunities to kill two birds with one stone everywhere I looked. For instance, I loved getting pedicures, but they seemed like a waste of precious time. So what if I let myself get one only when I had a reading assignment I needed to do? I'd waste less time, while still having my toes buffed, massaged, and polished. And what if I let myself binge-watch my favorite Netflix TV shows only while folding laundry, cooking, doing the dishes, or completing other household chores? Years later, as a professor, I even realized I could eat less junk food if visits to my favorite burger joint were reserved for mentoring sessions with a difficult student I knew I should see more often. I'd spend more time mentoring to get the burgers I craved but eat fewer of them overall. I called this strategy "temptation bundling," and I started applying it wherever I could.

Naturally, as a budding behavioral scientist, I wanted to know whether temptation bundling might be useful not just to me but to other people, too. And as an assistant professor at Wharton, I cooked up a scheme to test that possibility.

Right across the street from my office at Wharton is Pottruck Fitness Center, the University of Pennsylvania's premier gym. After I lined up the funding and collaborators I'd need to scientifically test the value of temptation bundling,* I papered Penn's campus with signs inviting anyone in the community who wanted to exercise more at Pottruck and who owned an iPod to sign up for a study and earn 100 dollars. In exchange, all they'd have to do was spend an hour under my direction at the gym at the outset of the semester and let my team access data about their gym visits for the remainder of the academic year.

Unsurprisingly, hundreds of eager students and staff signed up. What could be better than earning 100 dollars and getting a little help kick-starting improved exercise habits?

When the study participants showed up for their initial visits at Pottruck, we had even more good news for them. We'd be offering them gifts on top of their 100-dollar payment. But just what those gifts were and how they could be used was varied.

We loaned some people iPods preloaded with four tempting audio

---

*The amazing Julia Minson and Kevin Volpp partnered with me on this project.

novels of their choice (books we'd prescreened to ensure they were enticing, such as *The Hunger Games* and *The Da Vinci Code*). After receiving their gift, the study participants worked out while listening to the opening of an audio novel they'd picked. And then they learned that if they wanted to find out what happened next in their book, they would have to come back to the gym, where their loaned iPod would remain in a locked, monitored locker. They would be allowed to listen to their audiobooks only while exercising. The logic of the experiment was immediately obvious to everyone—we hoped this temptation would help lure people back to the gym for more workouts.

A second "control" group of study participants was also encouraged to exercise more and required to complete a workout at the beginning of our study. But instead of receiving a loaned iPod containing audio novels they could access only at the gym, these Penn students and staff were given a gift certificate to Barnes and Noble. Since they already owned iPods,* they could have used this cash to load their devices with audio content if they so desired, but we didn't suggest it, and few of them did.

As we'd expected, the participants who had been given the opportunity to temptation bundle were much more frequent gym visitors than those in the control group. In the week after students and staff enrolled in our study, the ones given loaned iPods exercised 55 percent more than members of our study's control group. What's more, they saw substantial benefits for seven weeks—the weeks leading up to the university's Thanksgiving break. Temptation bundling had real value after all.

But the most intriguing discovery we made in this study was *who*

---

*Recall that owning an iPod was a prerequisite for joining our study.

got the biggest benefits from temptation bundling. It turned out that the people we'd found it hardest to schedule for an initial workout—those whose lives were packed with many commitments—increased their exercise most when they were able to bundle gym visits with a tempting audiobook.

Though we hadn't anticipated this last finding, my collaborators and I immediately saw the logic in it. It was, in fact, my own busy life that led me to dream up the idea to temptation bundle in the first place, and it had proven enormously helpful to me back in graduate school.* Those of us with hectic schedules are exactly the people you'd expect to most need a strong lure to get to the gym (or accomplish any other everyday goal). For us, relying solely on willpower to get things done is particularly hopeless because we have so little energy left at the end of a long day.

The study also had a disappointing revelation, however. The effectiveness of temptation bundling dissipated after seven weeks, when Pottruck gym shut down for Thanksgiving break (an example of a disruptive fresh start). This discovery inspired a follow-up project. In partnership with Audible and 24 Hour Fitness gyms, my collaborators and I developed a new, monthlong program that was offered to thousands of gym members hoping to exercise more.† Some people who signed up for the program were simply encouraged to work out more (they were the "control" group), but others received a free audiobook download, were taught about temptation bundling, and were advised

---

*I became a regular exerciser, developed the focus to ace even my toughest classes (with fewer tempting distractions at home), and got to enjoy all of the *Harry Potter* books and most of the *Alex Cross* series in the bargain.

†This team was led by my fantastic PhD student Erika Kirgios.

to try restricting their enjoyment of audiobooks to times when they were exercising.

In this case, we found that giving people a free audiobook download and explaining temptation bundling led to a 7-percentage-point increase in the likelihood they'd squeeze in at least one workout each week during the monthlong program. It also led to a sustained boost in the likelihood of weekly exercise for at least seventeen weeks after our intervention ended (at which point we stopped collecting follow-up data, so the benefits might have been even longer-lasting). Though nowhere near as impressive as the 55 percent initial boost in exercise spurred by holding people's audiobooks in a secure gym locker, the success of this intervention was still exciting because it involved only a suggestion; we didn't limit anyone's behavior, as we had by physically confining their iPods in the first study. And it confirmed that temptation bundling can change behavior in a robust, lasting way.

The moral of this research to me is that temptation bundling certainly works best if you can actually restrict an indulgence to whenever you're doing a task that requires an extra boost of motivation (such as making it possible to listen to audiobooks *only* at the gym, and not in your car or on the bus). But merely *suggesting* that people try temptation bundling is enough to produce benefits that last.

More recent research in one Florida high school indicates that bundling temptations with the good-for-us behaviors that we sometimes dread can increase not just long-term persistence on the things we know we should do, but also short-term persistence. Much to the surprise of many teachers who feared it would be distracting, when students were given the opportunity to enjoy snacks, music, and Magic Markers while working on challenging math worksheets, they got more of their assignment done.

Happily, when temptation bundling works, tough goals are dreaded no longer and wasted time can be recovered in the bargain. And I've learned bundling can be used to solve all kinds of problems ranging from making more home-cooked meals (no wine unless you're at the stove) to finishing projects (by, say, reserving podcast listening for scrapbooking time).

Unfortunately, not all activities can be bundled with one another. For instance, responding to all the new emails in my inbox requires my full attention, so combining that task with an audiobook, podcast, or TV show is not an option. In general, a cognitively demanding task can't easily be paired with another cognitively demanding task. And the same applies to physically demanding activities: burger eating or wine drinking won't work in a bundle with exercise. These complexities mean temptation bundling can't *always* help you tackle present bias when you're pursuing change. It's just one tool to consider.

It's also not a fail-safe strategy for helping *other* people change, since it asks people to police themselves. If they aren't fully on board, they can easily cheat (enjoying temptations unbundled!). What are your options then?

MAKING WORK FUN

In 2012, Jana Gallus, a brilliant young economist studying for her doctorate at the University of Zurich, became intrigued by a problem that was plaguing Wikipedia, the fifty-million-entry online encyclopedia available in more than 280 languages. The site's top performing new editors were leaving in droves.

What made this challenge so interesting to Jana is that the editors—the so-called Wikipedians who keep the site's articles on everything from *Game of Thrones* to quantum mechanics accurate and up-to-date—don't get paid a dime. So cash rewards couldn't be used to solve the problem.

The organization's reliance on a volunteer labor force made it the perfect petri dish for exploring alternatives to money as a means of motivating people to achieve their full potential. This was a somewhat unusual topic for an economist to pursue, since economic theory generally assumes cash is king. But Jana's own experience had taught her that people care about much more than cash rewards. Enjoyment and the prospect of earning recognition from colleagues had often proven far more motivating to her than a paycheck. She was eager to prove this to others in her profession and contribute to a growing body of research countering economic models that neglect such nonmonetary sources of motivation. Having built an empire on the backs of volunteer labor, Wikipedia seemed like the ideal place to explore her theory.

Jana saw an opportunity both to advance her research and to help an inspiring organization. She also recognized Wikipedia's struggle to keep its editors engaged with the sometimes monotonous task of curating online content as another symptom of present bias. In short, persisting on dull tasks without the allure of immediate rewards is a pain. Just as this fact of life can pose a challenge for those of us trying to achieve our personal goals, it can also be a hindrance for organizations. The work they need completed isn't always instantly gratifying.

Eager to learn more about Wikipedia's problem, Jana started attending monthly roundtable gatherings of local Wikipedians to gather intel about the organization's turnover issues. These were official get-togethers held in restaurants and museums by small groups of passionate volunteer editors eager to talk about their areas of expertise and their community as a whole. It wasn't long before she had befriended several prominent contributors and learned both about their editorial work (one was an expert on Iceland, another on trains) and the crux of the retention challenge their community faced. As she immersed herself in their world, Jana became convinced that she could reduce turnover with a small zero-cost change to Wikipedia's platform.

When she told her newfound friends what she had in mind, the promise was too good to pass up: The Wikipedia leaders in her community agreed to let Jana run an experiment with four thousand new volunteer editors.

Based on the flip of a coin, Jana told some deserving Wikipedia newcomers that they had earned an accolade for their efforts, and their names were listed as award winners on a Wikipedia website. (Wikipedia selected winners based on how frequently editors contributed and the durability of their posts.*) The outstanding volunteers given honors also received either one, two, or three stars, which appeared next to their username, with more stars allocated to better performers. Other newcomers who had contributed equally valuable content to Wikipedia but came out on the other end of the coin flip received no symbolic awards (and were not alerted that such awards existed).

Jana hypothesized that the awards would make a monotonous

---

*Note that error-riddled posts are quickly tweaked by other Wikipedians, but a post that endures unchanged is presumed to be high-quality. Durability means no one else has taken issue with the veracity of a post's content.

task feel a bit more like a game. They didn't change the nature of the work itself but simply added an element of fun and praise for a job well done.

You can probably guess that Jana's experiment was a success (or else why would I be sharing this story?), but what you might not guess is that it helped *tremendously*. The results of Jana's project were stunning: The volunteers who received recognition for their efforts were 20 percent more likely to volunteer for Wikipedia again in the following month than those of equal caliber who earned no praise for their work. And, amazingly, this gap in engagement had remarkable staying power—the volunteers who earned symbolic awards were 13 percent more likely than others to be active on Wikipedia a year later.

Jana's experiment with Wikipedia is an example of something called "gamification," or the act of making an activity that isn't a game feel more engaging and less monotonous by adding gamelike features such as symbolic rewards, a sense of competition, and leaderboards. Gamification was much hyped by business consultants about a decade ago as a strategy that organizations could use to more effectively motivate employees, not by changing the work itself but by changing the packaging of the work, thus making goal achievement a bit more exciting ("Yes! I earned a star!"). For example, Cisco, a technology conglomerate, gamified a program intended to help its employees acquire social media skills, offering badges as rewards when trainees reached different levels in their certification classes. Similarly, Microsoft created leaderboards to gamify the verification of language translations in its global products. And the global software company SAP created a game that awarded badges to employees and placed them on leaderboards based on their sales performance.

On the face of it, gamification might seem like a no-brainer: Why wouldn't a corporation want to make work more fun? But as a top-down strategy for behavior change it can easily backfire, as two of my Wharton colleagues discovered. Like Jana, Ethan Mollick and Nancy Rothbard were excited about the potential for gamification to revolutionize productivity, so they ran an experiment a few years ago with several hundred salespeople whose jobs were somewhat boring. These salespeople were responsible for reaching out to local businesses and convincing them to offer coupons for discounted products or services that were then sold on their company's local website (think Groupon). The salespeople earned commissions for each coupon eventually sold online.

In an attempt to make these sales jobs more exciting, Ethan and Nancy worked with professional game designers to create a basketball-themed sales game. In the game, salespeople could earn points by closing deals with customers, with more points awarded for bigger deals. Sales from warm leads were called "layups," while cold calls were dubbed "jump shots." Giant screens on the sales floor displayed the names of top performers and showed occasional basketball animations like a successful dunk. Regular emails updated the "players" on who was winning, and when the game was over the winner got a bottle of champagne.

To test the effects of this game on employees' performance, Ethan and Nancy allowed employees on just one sales floor to participate; employees on the company's other two sales floors were left out. They then compared the trajectories of salespeople who played the game with those who didn't.

Though they'd had high hopes, Ethan and Nancy were surprised to find that playing the game didn't improve sales performance, and it also didn't improve the way salespeople felt at work. That said, digging into their data further did show a very interesting pattern.

My colleagues had asked everyone in their game a set of questions to determine whether they had "bought in" to it. Did people follow the game? Did they understand the rules? Did they think it was fair? These questions were designed to measure which salespeople had "entered the magic circle," a term used to describe agreeing to be bound by a game's rules rather than the normal rules that guide our daily interactions.* If people haven't entered the magic circle, there's no real point to a game. When I play Monopoly with my young son, for instance, he's not entering the magic circle when he simply steals all the money from the bank. And that means the game isn't much fun for him—there's no real point, no real challenge.

Ethan and Nancy found the same principle applied in their study. The salespeople who felt that the basketball game was a load of baloney (and thus didn't want to play by the rules) actually felt worse about work after the game was introduced, and their sales performance declined slightly.† The game benefited only the salespeople who had fully bought in to it (they became significantly more upbeat at work).

Ethan and Nancy believe that their study highlights a common mistake companies make with gamification. Gamification is unhelpful and can even be harmful if people feel that their employer is forcing them to participate in "mandatory fun." And if a game is a dud

---

*The origin of the concept is attributed to Dutch historian Johan Huizinga, who wrote on the play element in culture in 1938, but Eric Zimmerman and Katie Salen popularized the term in their 2003 book, *Rules of Play*, about game design and gamification.

†The drop in sales performance was what scientists call "marginally significant," which basically means that while performance moved down on average, whether it was a meaningful drop or a statistical aberration is somewhat ambiguous.

(and it's a bit of an art to create a game that isn't), it doesn't do anyone any good. It would be like temptation bundling your workout with a boring lecture.

WHAT'S POSSIBLE WITH BUY-IN

While Ethan and Nancy's experiment was a disappointment, gamification isn't always a wash. At its best, gamification helps people achieve goals they want to reach anyway by making the *process* more exciting. The important thing is that everyone playing the game elects to be there. When people do buy in, the results can be impressive.

Consider the experience of Nancy Strahl, who made an appearance on my podcast to explain how gamification changed her life. Nancy's world was turned upside down in 2008 when she started feeling nauseous after dropping her husband and son at the airport. She assumed it was food poisoning, but when her condition worsened and she finally went to the hospital, Nancy learned she was having a stroke. When she woke up a day later, her doctors explained that the left side of her body had been paralyzed. She was unlikely to recover fully and would probably never walk again.

But still, there was a chance. And Nancy was prepared to do everything she could to regain independence—she hoped to dance at her sons' weddings and help take care of her future grandchildren. Unfortunately, she learned that regaining mobility would require sticking to an intense, long-term rehabilitation program.

Determined to succeed, Nancy started doing five hours of inpatient rehab a day, but eventually her hospital stay ended and it was up to her to plow through the exercises on her own. She'd need to push herself each day at home through dozens of maneuvers provided by a physical therapist, which would be challenging and dull. No surprise, compliance tends to be very poor with these kinds of programs. The odds were good that Nancy wouldn't get far.

In her search for a path forward, Nancy stumbled upon a clinical trial testing a new kind of rehab program—one that involved a video game. Her exercises were embedded in a white water rafting adventure called "Recovery Rapids." Each day, she climbed into a virtual kayak and paddled down an on-screen river, picking up bottles or finding a treasure chest and winding her way through rapids. When Nancy mastered one level, the game got harder. And quickly, she was hooked—the game was not only tremendously fun, but she was noticing its benefits. She'd play and then realize she'd been able to turn the lights on by herself for the first time since her stroke.

Nancy made an astonishing recovery. Slowly, she regained the ability to walk and drive, and she even took up kayaking on a lake near her house. Several years after her doctors told her she'd never walk again, she danced at her son's wedding.

Today Nancy has the independence she feared she'd lost forever in her stroke. And she credits a gamified approach to recovery with her success.

Nancy's case isn't unique—science suggests gamification can help many of us tackle our goals, so long as we're choosing to use it to pursue goals we *want* to achieve. Consider a twelve-week experiment run with families in Massachusetts hoping to exercise more, some of whom had their exercise "gamified." Every family in this experiment set daily step-count goals and received daily feedback on their success hitting those goals (participants wore digital activity trackers). But some *also* earned points for walking, had the chance to advance from one game level to the next if they accumulated enough points, and could win a coffee mug if they reached the highest level by the end of the game.

Although the grand prize was essentially symbolic (a coffee mug is nice, but it isn't going to pay the bills), gamification still had big benefits. During the game and, more impressively, for twelve weeks after it ended, the families randomly assigned to play exercised far more than those whose exercise had not been gamified. Just as Recovery Rapids made Nancy Strahl's rehab more fun, the game made exercise more enjoyable, so people did more of it, and the change to their activity levels stuck.

More important, all participants *volunteered* for this and willingly "entered the magic circle." It's become clear the Mary Poppins approach helps us the most when we're already eager to help ourselves.

While this means we can set ourselves up for success, it leaves a burning question. How can *managers* take advantage of gamification, if they can't assume that employees will want to buy in? One low-risk way to make work more appealing is to simply make the workplace itself more enticing and fun—it's rare for employees to object to that. Consider Google's pioneering and widely imitated office design, which stunned me on my 2012 visit. The company offers employees all the trappings of a luxury resort: free and delicious food, Ping-Pong tables, lap pools, volleyball courts, and T-shirt giveaways. Or take Asana— a tech company that gives its employees a 10,000-dollar budget to decorate their workspaces. Or The Farmer's Dog, a dog food company that "employs" dogs to keep human employees feeling loved and entertained (they even have official titles: Chief Inspirational Officer and Head of Playtime). The list goes on and on—innovative companies all around us are busy using the Mary Poppins approach to make their employees' experiences at work more fun. When the coronavirus pandemic forced most U.S. employees to start working remotely, companies even found ways to make telecommuting more fun. Virtual happy hours became all the rage at companies like Zappos; some even got cute with meetup names like "Quaran-tinis."

Although some employers are wise to it, I think the real wonder is that so many of us fail to adopt Mary Poppins's advice. To "get it," we first have to acknowledge that, much of the time, it's *not* conveniently the case that we love doing what's good for us. Instead, the beastliest impediments to change are often the short-term pain and inconvenience associated with doing what we know we should do. Typically, when we pursue ambitious goals, we're working against the tug of temptation.

But as I've happily discovered since my graduate school days of linking James Patterson novels with exercise, there's a simple solution. We just need to "flip the script" so that instant gratification is working for us, not against us. Research has proven time and again that rather than relying on willpower to resist temptation, we're better off figuring out how to make good behaviors more gratifying in the short-term. Big payoffs far down the road just aren't enough to keep us motivated. The Mary Poppins approach takes the fun that might typically distract us from our goals and uses it to transform an obstacle into an enticement—suddenly we *want* to go to the gym, focus at work, eat a healthier diet, and study harder. That kind of desire is a powerful motivator for change.

Chapter Takeaways

- Present bias (a.k.a. impulsivity)—the tendency to favor instantly gratifying temptations over larger long-term rewards—is a pernicious obstacle to change.

- Mary Poppins has it right. When goal pursuit is made instantly gratifying by adding "an element of fun," present bias can be overcome.

- Temptation bundling entails allowing yourself to engage in a guilty pleasure (such as binge-watching TV) only when pursuing a virtuous or valuable activity that you tend to dread (such as exercise).

- Temptation bundling solves two problems at once. It can help reduce overindulgence in temptations and increase time spent on activities that serve your long-term goals.

- Gamification is another way to make goal pursuit instantly gratifying. It involves making something that isn't a game feel more engaging and less monotonous by adding gamelike features such as symbolic rewards, a sense of competition, and leaderboards.

- Gamification works when players "buy in" to the game. It can backfire if players feel the game is being imposed on them.

CHAPTER 3

Procrastination

I n 2002, Omar Andaya was the president of Green Bank, one of the largest retail banks in the Philippines. And he faced a challenge common to banking executives: his customers weren't saving enough money.

A few years earlier, when Omar took the bank's helm from his ailing father, he became aware of this problem. It bothered him immensely for two reasons. First, he recognized that undersaving has dire consequences—it limits access to health care, stunts educational achievement, and ultimately limits a person's earnings potential. Second, customers with meager savings were bad for his bank's finances. Fixing the problem would help his customers *and* his business. So he started brainstorming possible solutions.

But the thing is, getting people to save more money is really, really hard. Even in the United States, which is much wealthier than the Philippines, one in three families in 2015 had no money saved whatsoever, and 41 percent of families would have been unable to cover an unexpected 2000-dollar expense. Around the time Omar took over Green Bank, about 31 percent of all families in the Philippines fell below the poverty line. A really hard challenge was not going to dissuade Omar, but he wasn't sure what to do.

So he was excited when in 2002 a friend put him in touch with Nava Ashraf, Dean Karlan, and Wesley Yin, three academics who studied consumers in developing economies and who had a proposal for how to increase Green Bank customers' savings rates.*

There was just one small problem. A lot of people who heard their pitch thought it was crazy.

The academics told Omar that he should give his customers the opportunity to put their savings in a "locked" bank account—an idea that had been refined through extensive focus grouping. This kind of account would be the same as other savings accounts Green Bank offered, earning the same interest rate. But it would come with an important twist: customers who chose it would be forbidden from taking money out of the account until a future date they selected or until they reached a self-selected balance. The accounts would be like financial chastity belts.

Each year, in a class I teach to about 150 Wharton MBA students, I share Omar's story. And when I explain this proposal, things inevitably get interesting. My students begin to argue about its merits. The ones who've studied economics for years can't help but gasp. Why would anyone put their money into a bank account they can't access at will without a great incentive, like a high interest rate? To them, the accounts sound outrageous—a transparent scam to keep

---

*Mary Kay Gugerty also worked on the ideation phase of this project but later dropped off the team.

people from their hard-earned cash. And these students do have a point. Locked accounts ignore a basic economic principle; namely, that people prefer flexibility over constraints and freedom over penalties.

Many of Omar's colleagues at Green Bank had the same concern as my skeptical students. But Omar was desperate to try something, and he saw a spark of psychological insight in this outlandish proposal—the same insight that another group of Wharton MBAs inevitably notices, too, igniting a fierce class debate each year. So in 2003, after much backing-and-forthing with his colleagues, Omar decided to take a calculated risk on locked accounts. He would let the academics who'd pitched the new savings product offer it to a few hundred Green Bank customers as an experiment, and they'd see what happened.

TACKLING PROCRASTINATION

Around the time that Omar was contemplating the rollout of an unusual new type of bank account in the Philippines, a behavioral scientist at the Massachusetts Institute of Technology (MIT) named Dan Ariely was struggling to understand a different but related problem. He couldn't believe how often his students procrastinated on class assignments. These were some of the best students in the world, and it bothered him to no end that they let "temptation take them on a date, over to the student union for a meeting, and off on a ski trip in the mountains—while their workload fell farther and farther behind." He suspected that his students were learning less than they would if they could buckle down and focus on their work when it was assigned rather than right before it was due. As a fellow professor, I can relate. It's infuriating when brilliant students shoot themselves in the foot by missing class deadlines that I know they could meet if they'd just stay focused.

Dan was so perplexed by his students' poor study habits that he decided to team up with his colleague Klaus Wertenbroch to run some experiments to learn more about their behavior. The duo had a hunch that they might be able to help MIT whiz kids help themselves, and in the bargain, learn something about how people manage to achieve their goals in the face of the temptation to procrastinate.

Dan and Klaus began by running a study with ninety-nine MIT students who were about to start a fourteen-week class with Dan. To pass the course, each student would have to hand in three short papers. About half the students would be given deadlines for their assignments, evenly spaced out throughout the term. But Dan gave the other half of his students an unusual opportunity. He told them they wouldn't be required to turn in any of the three papers until the last day of class. However, if they wanted, they could select earlier deadlines of their own choosing for each paper. If they missed their self-set deadlines, Dan would lower their grades for each day they were late.

Now, it's worth pointing out that much like opening a locked bank account, voluntarily choosing a deadline with a lateness penalty violates a basic tenet of economic theory, which states that people should always prefer more freedom over less. That general preference for flexibility is why your airline can charge you a huge premium for a changeable airline ticket, why restaurants can put a higher price tag on their brunch buffets than on their heartiest à la carte offerings, and why banks generally give you a higher interest rate on certificates of deposit that have fixed withdrawal dates than on a savings account that can be tapped at any time.

Yet Dan was, in effect, asking his students to pay a premium for a *lack* of flexibility. From the perspective of a classically trained economist, the best strategy for Dan's students would be to reject his proffered deadlines and allow themselves as much time as possible to finish each paper. This would maximize their flexibility to deal with work due in other classes and additional commitments without incurring any penalties.

But 68 percent of Dan's students chose the restrictive option. They *wanted* the deadlines.

When I share this fact with my MBA students, it inevitably revives the debate that began with the story about Omar Andaya and Green Bank. Many of my students argue that Dan's data show MIT students aren't so smart after all. If they're willing to voluntarily adopt deadlines with penalties, they're making a clear mistake. In school, where you're bombarded with deadlines in every class, students should value flexibility and freedom. But other students in my class ardently disagree. They point to the challenge of time management and note that binding deadlines make it easier to space work out evenly throughout the term (rather than discovering, as finals approach, that there is more to do than can possibly be done well).

This debate only intensifies when I reveal to my students that Dan's findings have good company. In the Philippines, Nava, Dean, and Wesley found that 28 percent of Green Bank customers who were offered locked bank accounts chose them over standard, unlocked accounts or no account at all. (Twenty-eight percent is by no means a landslide, but it's an enormous figure if you think the number should be zero.)

At this point in my class, students with extensive training in economics are practically ripping out their hair. They insist it's crazy for people to voluntarily lock away their money without an interest rate premium or sign up for class deadlines with penalties. People should never want to give up flexibility or freedom without being compensated for it! This isn't just a central tenet of economic theory or a cornerstone of government policy and marketing strategies the world over (there's a reason cruise ships and resorts flaunt their all-inclusive, all-you-can-eat offerings). It's also just common sense, right?

Maybe. But maybe not. In the previous chapter, I described how our impulsivity can be a big obstacle to achieving our goals, and I suggested that one solution is to turn impulsivity into an asset—by making virtuous behaviors fun. But when it comes to preventing procrastination, dangling a carrot is just one option; we can also use the stick. That is, we can see temptation coming a mile away and take steps to prevent our bad impulses from getting the best of us. That's what those Green Bank customers and students of Dan Ariely were doing: by opting into constraints—on when they could access their money, on how much they could procrastinate—they were making it harder to give in to future temptations and easier to reach their long-term goals.

HANDCUFFING OURSELVES

The idea for Green Bank's locked accounts didn't come out of nowhere. History is littered with stories of people (mythical and real) who relied on similar techniques to resist temptation. Perhaps most famously, in *The Odyssey*, Odysseus asks to be bound to the mast of his ship so he won't succumb to the temptation of the Sirens' song and steer his ship off course.* My favorite example features the French writer Victor Hugo, an enthusiastic socialite who procrastinated on completing a first draft of *The Hunchback of Notre Dame*. Desperate to meet a strict deadline from his publisher, he locked up all his clothes except a shawl to cover himself. In so doing, he ensured he couldn't go out and about. Forced to stay home and focus on his novel, he successfully hit his deadline.

More than a hundred years later, academics became intrigued by people's odd tendency to self-impose constraints. In 1955, an economist named Robert Strotz noted that a subset of people (like Hugo) did peculiar things to keep themselves from indulging in impulses that would undermine their goals, such as contributing to special Christmas savings accounts throughout the year that didn't allow withdrawals before the holiday season or getting married in order to force themselves to "settle down" (remember, this paper came out in the 1950s).

Robert Strotz's article on the topic turned out to be a blockbuster (well, if any academic article can ever be called blockbuster). It introduced the heretical idea to economists that rather than always preferring flexibility and freedom, sometimes people want just the opposite because they know it will help them avoid temptation. Strotz's disciples (including the future economics Nobel laureates Thomas Schelling and Richard Thaler) began exploring these strategies in greater detail and gave a name to them: "commitment devices."

---

*At one point in Homer's epic adventure story, the hero—Odysseus—fears that he and his ship's crew will be tempted to redirect their vessel toward a deadly island inhabited by Sirens when they hear the Sirens' sweet voices calling to them from across the sea. To avoid this fate, Odysseus asks his crew to bind him to the mast and plug their ears with wax so no one will be able to give in to the anticipated temptation.

Whenever you do something that reduces your own freedoms in the service of a greater goal, you're using a commitment device. Telling your boss you'll finish an optional report by a certain date is a commitment device to get that work done. A traditional piggy bank— the ceramic kind that you have to break open if you want to access the money inside—is a commitment device that makes it ever-so-slightly harder to dip into your savings. Stocking your kitchen with small plates is a commitment device to help you eat smaller portions. Downloading an app like Moment that lets you set daily limits on your smartphone use is a commitment device aimed at reducing your technology addiction. And at the extreme, putting your name on a gambling self-exclusion list (an option in some states, like Pennsylvania) so you'll be arrested if you set foot in a casino is a commitment device to keep you away from the card tables.

Of course, restrictions designed to prevent impulsive choices are all around us: speed limits, laws against drug use, laws against texting while driving, and even standard, spaced-out homework deadlines. But normally these kinds of restrictions are imposed on us by a presumably benevolent third party, such as a government or a teacher. What makes commitment devices weird is that they're self-imposed— we're handcuffing *ourselves*!

While I hope I've given you at least some intuition for why handcuffing yourself from time to time could be useful, I've yet to give you any concrete evidence that these strategies work. So let me take you back to the locked savings accounts at Green Bank and the self-set deadlines in Dan Ariely's class and explain how they turned out.

The economists who pitched the idea for atypical bank accounts to Omar Andaya evaluated them through a large, carefully crafted study. They randomly assigned more than a thousand former or current Green Bank customers to one of two different groups. The first group, about eight hundred customers, was invited by the bank to open a locked account; the second group, roughly five hundred customers, was the "control" group, meaning that they received no such invitation. Then the researchers tracked everyone's savings balances over the next year (regardless of whether they opted for the locked account or not) to see if merely having the *choice* to open a locked bank account made a difference.

When the results came back, Dean Karlan, one of the study's leaders, told me he was floored. Compared with the control group, those offered locked accounts saved *80 percent more* over the next year. In other words, if a customer in the control group saved 100 dollars, a comparable customer with access to a locked account saved 180 dollars. That's a really big difference! The numbers are even more impressive when you consider that only 28 percent of customers offered access to locked accounts actually opened one. That means a relatively small number of people in the group offered locked accounts saved so much money that they vastly boosted the savings of the whole population.

This unorthodox idea was pretty clever after all; it really did help people achieve their savings goals.* But what about the costly deadlines Dan Ariely thought to offer his students?

Well, Dan and Klaus conducted a follow-up to the study I mentioned earlier in order to find out. This time, they compared how well a group of sixty MIT students performed on assignments when they

---

*It's worth noting that another experimental group was merely prompted to set goals and encouraged to save more without a locked account. This also moved account balances in the right direction, but the benefits were only about a third as big as the ones realized by those invited to open a commitment account.

either faced a single final deadline or could self-impose intermediate deadlines with late penalties.* As it turned out, students who could choose to self-impose deadlines handed in work that had about 50 percent fewer errors than the students who were randomly assigned to face a single final deadline. The opportunity to self-impose deadlines proved enormously useful, much like having access to a locked savings account.

To this day, I find the magnitude of these successes staggering and always enjoy sharing them with my MBA students, particularly the ones who argued adamantly that no one in their right mind would ever adopt—let alone benefit from—a commitment device.

The data are clear. Even if they do contradict a golden rule of economic theory, commitment devices can be something of a godsend. They help us change our behavior for the better by locking us into choices we make when we're clearheaded about what's good for us, not when we're hotheadedly reacting to an imminent temptation, and they keep us from indulging in the temptation to misbehave later on.

That's all well and good, a skeptic might note—but what if, say, your bank doesn't offer a locked savings account (almost no banks do)? How are you supposed to find a commitment device for every long-term goal you want to pursue? If you're an entrepreneur who wants to hit her deadlines, there's no teacher around to impose penalties for lateness. If you want to exercise more, I'm not likely to be at your gym handing out iPods loaded with audiobooks you can listen

---

*Recall that the previous study by Dan and Klaus that I mentioned had a different design—it compared students who had evenly spaced deadlines with those who could self-set deadlines.

to only on-site. For most goals you want to pursue, you'd be justified in wishing for a simple way to create your own commitment device.

Fortunately, there *is* a simple way.

CASH COMMITMENT DEVICES

Picture a big, juicy cheeseburger. It's loaded with your favorite toppings—lettuce, tomato, onion, bacon, whatever you crave most— and it smells incredible. If you were out to lunch with a friend and a waiter served that burger at the table next to yours, wouldn't you want one?

But what if you had just promised yourself you'd start eating healthier. Could you resist?

This is the question posed to my Wharton MBAs every year by guest speaker Jordan Goldberg. Jordan is a cofounder of stickK, the company whose data Hengchen, Jason, and I analyzed to determine whether people are more likely to set goals after fresh start dates.

After Jordan prompts my students to contemplate his burger scenario, the room invariably fills with murmurs. My students would all *like* to believe they'd have the willpower to resist, but most know themselves well enough to admit they *might* order the burger.

Next, Jordan asks an easier question: Now what if you knew you'd owe someone 500 dollars if you ate the cheeseburger? You'd think a lot harder about giving in to the tasty temptation, right?

Everyone nods, myself included. There's nothing controversial about that decision.

With these questions, Jordan has introduced my students to an unusual type of commitment device—one that helps you stick to your plans by literally making you pay if you don't. I call these "cash commitment devices," and there are several companies that offer them to consumers. To date, hundreds of thousands of people have given cash commitment devices a try, and they turn out to be quite handy. All you have to do is set a goal, choose someone (or some piece of technology) to accurately track your progress, and put money on the line that you'll have to forfeit to a third party if you don't succeed. (You can specify if you'd like the money to go to a certain individual or charity, and to ensure failing will really sting, you can even pick a charity you hate—an "anti-charity"—such as a gun rights or gun control group, depending on your politics.) You can wager as little as a few bucks, but bigger stakes, unsurprisingly, correlate with higher rates of success.

Want to make it to your house of worship more regularly? Name a reliable patron as your referee and put money on the line in case you fail to go. Want to date fewer losers? Pick a friend with good taste to hold you accountable and set the stakes.*

Not long ago, I spoke with the author and tech entrepreneur Nick Winter, who used a cash commitment device to help change his life path. Back in 2012, at the age of twenty-six, Nick was a software coder who felt his life wasn't living up to his expectations. Dissatisfied and frustrated, he asked himself, "What can I do to make life more well-rounded, more fulfilling? What would be exciting? How do I want to live?"

As he mulled over these questions, Nick told me, he realized his day-to-day sorely lacked adventure. Sure, he loved writing code, and his job was fulfilling, but the most exciting thing he'd done lately was

---

*Admittedly a few losers might slip through the cracks, as they can be hard to detect.

hit the gym. Nick's second revelation was that he wasn't using the artistic side of his brain enough. He wanted to do something more creative.

Fueled by these revelations, Nick resolved to transform himself into a wide-ranging adventurer—skydiving, learning to skateboard, learning to lucid dream, lowering his 5K time by five minutes, and much, much more—and to write a book about his transformation. He gave himself three months to do everything.

Now, Nick was under no illusions. He realized it would be hard to accomplish such a big life change in such a short time. And he was pretty sure that just announcing his plans to his friends wouldn't be enough (though that's where he started, so he'd at least feel ashamed if he didn't make any progress). He was confident that to achieve his goals, he'd need to set the stakes higher. So he was intrigued when he heard about a company that would sell him a very unusual kind of contract. It worked like this: Nick agreed to pay an enormous fine— roughly 14,000 dollars—if he *didn't* write a book and go skydiving in three months.*

Maybe 14,000 dollars would be small change to a billionaire, but Nick wasn't rich. He was risking almost everything in his bank account, which, in his mind, gave him no choice but to write the book and jump off the plane.

Saddled with a huge incentive to get it done, in less than three months Nick wrote a (quite popular!) book about his adventuring: *The Motivation Hacker.* And he went skydiving with his girlfriend to boot—an accomplishment he's perhaps more proud of, given his life-long fear of heights.

---

*The fine would be just 7,000 dollars if he accomplished one goal but not the other.

I love Nick's story because it so nicely illustrates the power and simplicity of cash commitment devices. It also highlights a somewhat contradictory feature of cash commitment devices. On the one hand, when we use them, we're *flouting* the standard laws of economics, which say more freedom is better than less. But on the other hand, we're also *leaning heavily* on standard economics, which recommends that you hike up the price of unwanted behavior or impose restrictions to discourage it. These are the very solutions economics prescribes, such as taxing cigarettes and alcohol or banning marijuana to reduce consumption.

Cash commitments, like other incentives, are particularly handy because they are so versatile—far more so than other types of commitment devices that require, say, an app to lock your smartphone after too many hours of use or a casino that will deny you entry after you sign up for a self-exclusion list. You just need some money you don't want to lose and someone (or something) to monitor your progress.

Of course, a real problem is that cash commitment devices sound pretty bizarre to some people. After all, you're literally signing up to pay fines! But the thing is, they've proven highly effective even if they are counterintuitive. For instance, one study of two thousand smokers found that having access to a cash commitment device (in this case, a savings account in which they could deposit money they would recover only if they passed a nicotine urine test in six months) helped people quit. On average, the smokers who decided to use cash commitments made deposits roughly once every two weeks, contributing a total of about 20 percent of a month's income to the account they would lose if they didn't quit smoking. And remarkably, 30 percent more of the smokers who had the opportunity to risk their own cash to quit managed to do so. Similar cash commitment opportunities have been shown to help gym goers exercise more, dieters lose more weight, and families buy healthier groceries.

The biggest challenge with cash commitment devices isn't their effectiveness; it's getting more people comfortable with the idea of using them. And it's reasonable to have some hesitation. As great as these results sound, maybe you're just not ready to impose costly restrictions or fines on yourself in case you don't hit all of your goals. If so, you're not alone. Only 11 percent of smokers, for example, were willing to put any of their cash on the line to help them kick their nicotine habit.*

There are lots of likely reasons for this. One is that not everyone is interested in changing. Another is that even if you do want to change, sometimes failure is out of your control. What if, say, a family emergency arises, and prevents you from meeting your exercise goals? Then you'd be stuck dealing not only with that trauma, but also with the financial penalty from your commitment device. Maybe that possibility is just more than you can bear, period, full stop. What then?

PLEDGES AND OTHER SOFT COMMITMENTS

Imagine you're a busy doctor meeting with a patient who's complaining of a sore throat, stuffy nose, and cough. It's clear that all your patient wants is a prescription to put her out of her misery. Naturally, you're eager to help.

But let's say your patient is begging for antibiotics, and you know

---

*As with the Green Bank study, it's worth noting that this relatively small group was so successful at quitting that it boosted the quitting statistics for *all* the people who were offered the special savings account.

her symptoms strongly suggest a bad cold, not a bacterial infection like strep throat or pneumonia. It's *possible* it's an infection, and that antibiotics could help, but it's unlikely. On top of being almost certainly unhelpful in this case, antibiotics are expensive and sometimes lead to bad reactions such as rashes, diarrhea, and vomiting. Plus, the more they're prescribed, the faster antibiotic-resistant bacteria evolve, making future infections more difficult to treat.

So now you face a troubling decision over what to do. Could you resist the temptation to write your patient the script she requested? Or would you break with medical guidelines and give her what she wants, hoping that will make her feel better, though the evidence suggests otherwise?

Although we like to think of doctors as infallible, research shows that many regularly give in to the temptation to offer patients what they want. In fact, American adults receive an estimated forty-one million unnecessary antibiotic prescriptions annually at a cost of more than a billion dollars (and that's just the price for the drugs).

Aware of these troubling statistics, a creative team of doctors and behavioral scientists who knew about the power of commitment had an idea they thought could help.*

Normally, when you're asked to pursue a goal at work that you really care about (such as making better decisions in the face of demanding patients), you probably think it over in your head and convince yourself you can do it. Maybe you even discuss your goal with a few close friends, family members, or colleagues, but that's often where the preparation stops.

---

*This team included Daniella Meeker, Tara Knight, Mark Friedberg, Jeffrey Linder, Noah Goldstein, Craig Fox, Alan Rothfeld, Guillermo Diaz, and Jason Doctor.

The researchers hoping to stem unnecessary antibiotic prescriptions realized this and came up with an additional step that they hoped would make doctors even more likely than usual to think twice before caving in to patients' demands. They asked doctors to sign a formal pledge not to prescribe antibiotics unless they were necessary and then to display that pledge publicly in their waiting rooms.

The psychology the researchers were counting on to buoy this tactic works like this: as soon as you sign a commitment and post it on your wall, you've created a mental cost for writing an unnecessary prescription. If you're tempted to write that script, you'll now be hyperaware that doing so means breaking your word. After all, you signed your name to a framed letter promising not to do this very thing. In short, the "price" of prescribing an unnecessary antibiotic has gone up.

The team that developed this idea convinced the managers of five busy primary care clinics in Los Angeles to let them test it. Some of the doctors in these clinics were asked to sign and post a pledge in their waiting rooms stating that they were "dedicated to avoid prescribing antibiotics when they are likely to do more harm than good." Other doctors (in a "control" group) got no such request.

Over the course of the study nearly one thousand patients complaining of acute cold symptoms visited these doctors' offices. And the researchers found that asking doctors to sign and post the pledge cut inappropriate antibiotic prescriptions by about a third compared with the control group.

That figure is incredible. But what impresses me most is that so many doctors were influenced by their pledge even though breaking it had no monetary penalty. A pledge like this stands in stark contrast to cash commitments, locked bank accounts, and deadline penalties,

which I call "hard commitments" because they involve a more concrete cost. The clinician pledge is a prime example of what I call a
"soft commitment"—a commitment that comes with only a *psychological* price tag for failure.

Naturally, there are a wide range of costs we can impose on ourselves, or that others can impose on us, to help us achieve our goals.
These range from *soft penalties*, such as announcing our goals or
deadlines publicly so we'll suffer humiliation if we miss them, to *hard
penalties*, such as having to hand over cash should we fail. There are
also *soft restrictions* we can self-impose, such as eating from a smaller
plate or using a piggy bank, and *hard restrictions*, such as putting our
money in a locked savings account or accepting gym-only access to
your iPod.

As I've already mentioned, for good reason, not everyone is comfortable with the idea of a commitment device that imposes significant penalties for misbehavior or restricts future freedoms. If a
penalty is too big, it can be self-defeating. Those who can't stomach
the thought of hard commitments may do better with a different fla-
vor of commitment device.

Signing a pledge is a particularly soft form of commitment because the penalty is simply the guilt and discomfort you'll feel if you
break your word, to others or yourself. Being at odds with yourself,
which psychologists call "cognitive dissonance," is a surprisingly
powerful force first studied by Leon Festinger in the 1950s. People
often go to great lengths to avoid reckoning with their internal con-
tradictions. Cognitive dissonance can help explain why cults are so
hard to leave (after you've joined and invested so much of yourself,
it's difficult to admit that you're unhappy) and why smokers often

underestimate the health effects of their habit (if you believe you're intelligent and also have a nasty habit, cognitive dissonance pushes you to discount or ignore evidence that your habit is, indeed, nasty). Cognitive dissonance is also a handy tool we can harness to change behavior for good. By electing to make pledges and asking others to do the same, we can turn cognitive dissonance into a soft penalty that helps us and them achieve more.

Take a student of mine, Karen Herrera, as an example. When Karen arrived as a freshman at my university's Philadelphia campus, she was clinically obese and incredibly unhappy with her body. Now a junior, she's managed to lose forty unwanted pounds. How did she do it? She told me that within weeks of arriving on campus, she signed up for sessions with a nutritionist that changed everything. In each session, Karen made small, manageable, short-term diet and weight-loss commitments and plans for achieving them. Then, she visited her nutritionist to track her progress on a weekly basis. Over time, they developed a relationship. "Throughout the week, I'm making decisions and I don't want to let her down," Karen told me. "And I also don't want to let myself down." That desire not to let herself down (avoiding the pain of cognitive dissonance) or to disappoint her nutritionist (because she'd made a pledge) helped Karen achieve her goals. By the time I met her as a junior, she told me she felt amazing in her body for the first time, not to mention delighted with the enormous change she'd made and maintained—all thanks to a soft commitment.

It's worth noting that Karen's soft commitment was small and recurring. She wasn't pledging to lose forty pounds in one fell swoop but rather setting weekly, healthy, achievable weight-loss targets.

Lots of research on commitment supports the benefits of this "bite-size" approach.

Consider a study I helped conduct, led by my doctoral student Aneesh Rai, which involved thousands of volunteers at a large nonprofit who had promised to work two hundred hours within a year of joining but were falling short of their pledge. Knowing that facing such a massive goal can be demotivating, my collaborators and I instead asked the volunteers to commit to four hours each week or eight hours every two weeks—which, of course, is basically the same as two hundred hours a year. But these smaller commitments, despite amounting to the same annual pledge, yielded 8 percent more time volunteering overall than simply prompting people to make progress on a yearly commitment. (Likewise, the online financial services company Acorns has found that it's more effective when people are asked to set aside 5 dollars in savings daily rather than 35 dollars weekly or 150 dollars monthly even though these amount to the same thing.) If a commitment is bite-size, it appears less daunting to us, and we're more likely to stick to our word.

TWO TYPES OF PEOPLE

As much as I enjoy teaching my Wharton MBA students about commitment devices and sharing Omar's story, the debate it sparks also touches on a sore spot for me. When I first learned about research on hard commitment devices as a graduate student, I, too, felt disappointment and frustration. Unlike my MBA students, though, I was never held in any suspense as to the value of hard commitment devices. I was taught they worked before I ever had time to consider that some people might find them counterintuitive. As a result, my frustration wasn't about the existence of a product that defied a classic law of economics. Instead I was initially indignant about how *few* people use them. The data proved to me that these valuable tools should be wildly popular. Yet most people seem to find soft commitments more appealing than hard commitments, despite the fact that they lack the same pinch and so are substantially less effective.

It's not just that hard commitment devices are unpopular. It's that they strike many people—including a large fraction of my bright, business-savvy Wharton MBAs—as downright bizarre. Remember that not only Green Bank executives but also a substantial subset of their customers were originally skeptical of the value of locked accounts. Given the opportunity to open a locked account, 72 percent of customers declined to do so. And smokers hoping to quit were also dubious about using cash commitment devices: 89 percent refused to put money in a commitment account. Data from other studies paint a similar picture, suggesting that low rates of adoption are the norm. And as further evidence that commitment devices are not wildly popular, none of the leading cash commitment device companies (such as stickK and Beeminder) are hugely successful.

So what gives? Commitment devices are tremendously useful, and given how many of us struggle to achieve our goals, you'd think demand would be sky-high. The self-help industry is estimated to be a 10 billion dollars per year market. Clearly, people want help meeting their biggest, most challenging goals, yet they frequently take a pass on these enormously effective tools.

Behavioral economists studying commitment devices think they have a partial explanation, and it isn't that most people don't need these tools or even that they're worried about encountering an unforeseeable obstacle on the path to success. The theory is that there are two types of people in the world. Everyone has self-control problems, so that isn't the distinguishing characteristic. Rather, some of us have come to terms with our impulsivity and are willing to take steps to rein it in. Behavioral economists call these people "sophisticates." But not everyone in the world is a sophisticate, as evidenced by the debate that rages whenever I teach Wharton MBA students about Green Bank's unusual savings product. Lots of people are instead overly optimistic about their ability to overcome their self-control problems through sheer willpower. These types of people are "naïfs."*

While everyone would like to believe they're a sophisticate, the world is also, sadly, full of naïfs. Combined with some appropriate fear of costly failure, that's the best explanation we have for why so many people who could benefit from commitment devices aren't willing to use them. Naïfs haven't yet come to the realization that commitment devices, while strange sounding in theory, are incredibly useful tools for mastering their self-control problems. If this weren't the case, if the world were full of sophisticates, you would presumably see lots of people eagerly accepting—even demanding—commitment devices from their banks, gyms, teachers, and doctors. Also, if the world were full of sophisticates, offering people commitment devices would be enough to solve all their problems with temptation. If we were all sophisticates, then everyone who stood to benefit from commitment devices would use one, and anyone who miraculously didn't need help would pass. In such a world, we wouldn't need third-party

---

*Rhymes with "high leafs."

restrictions, such as laws forbidding drunk driving (instead, people could install Breathalyzers to prevent themselves from starting a vehicle inebriated) and requiring Social Security payments (people could just sign up for locked accounts to ensure they saved sufficient money).

Unfortunately, that's not the world we live in. Dan and Klaus showed in one of their studies, in fact, that giving MIT students the option to adopt deadlines with late penalties wasn't enough to help them do as well as possible on every assignment because many students who stood to benefit didn't agree to the commitment. They actually proved that their students would get better grades on their papers if they were *forced* to accept evenly spaced deadlines with late penalties, as students typically are. This and a great deal of other data suggest that many of us choose not to adopt commitment devices because we undervalue them or are naïve about how much we need them, not because we don't need them or are unwilling to risk the penalty.

The prevalence of naïfs suggests (not surprisingly) that one important function of a good manager is to set up systems that impose costs and restrictions on employees whenever temptation could stand in the way of wise long-term decisions. Such systems—such as deferring a subset of employee income into a pension plan or restricting access to certain websites at work—make commitment devices unnecessary because the right incentives already exist. "Good" commitments are already being imposed on employees by a third party.

Of course, such policies can be overly paternalistic. If your manager started imposing penalties for everything you did that she felt hindered your productivity or threatened your well-being, you'd feel micromanaged and mistrusted. We aren't always wrong to cherish the freedom to give in to temptation (and even enjoy it). A more restrictive organization isn't necessarily a better one.

If you're in the position of managing employees, imposing certain restrictions can be helpful when your employees have important goals to achieve and willpower is an obstacle. Maybe it's reasonable to block Facebook on company computers and take sodas out of vending machines. But you might also consider encouraging employees to set their own boundaries.

Savvy organizations often prompt employees or customers to make mutually beneficial commitments. For instance, a health care provider might encourage its customers to pledge to take life-saving pills a certain number of days per month (which my research has shown can significantly increase medication adherence). Or a manager can encourage employees to download software that limits time spent browsing social media or to voluntarily set deadlines for important assignments, or to adopt other kinds of commitments—be they public or private, penalized or costless. This is akin to what the researchers I described earlier did by prompting doctors to commit to reducing unnecessary antibiotic prescriptions.

That all said, we don't always have a benevolent organization, manager, researcher, policy maker, teacher, or parent looking over our shoulders. Fortunately, commitment devices can be quite useful when we're on our own: They let us incentivize ourselves. We just need to be sophisticated enough to recognize their value and put them to work.

The good news is that at this moment, you're in an enviable position. Having read this far, you're now a sophisticate (if you weren't one already). The last two chapters have armed you with the knowledge that self-control is a key obstacle to behavior change, causing

both impulsive decisions and procrastination, and you know commitment devices can rein in temptation before it has a chance to
knock you off track.

Chapter Takeaways

- Present bias often causes us to procrastinate on tasks that
  serve our long-term goals.

- An effective solution to this problem is to anticipate temptation and create constraints ("commitment devices") that
  disrupt this cycle. Whenever you do something that reduces
  your own freedoms in the service of a greater goal, you're
  using a commitment device. An example is a "locked" savings account that prevents you from accessing your money
  until you've reached your savings goal.

- Cash commitment devices are a versatile form of commitment device. They allow you to create a financial incentive
  to meet your goal by letting you put money on the line that
  you'll forfeit if you don't succeed.

- Public pledges are a form of "soft" commitment that increase the psychological cost of failing to meet your goals.
  They are surprisingly effective, though not as effective as
  "hard" commitments, which involve more tangible penalties or restrictions.

- The costs we can impose on ourselves to help with goal
  achievement range from soft penalties (such as announcing goals or deadlines publicly) to hard penalties (such as
  having to hand over cash should we fail). There are also

soft restrictions (such as eating from a smaller plate) and hard restrictions (such as putting our money in a locked savings account). The softer the penalty or restriction, the less likely it is to help with change, but the more palatable it is to adopt.

- Making smaller, more frequent commitments is more effective than making larger, less frequent ones, even when they amount to the same commitment (like saving 5 dollars a day as opposed to 1,825 dollars a year).

- Not everyone recognizes how much they could benefit from a commitment device. Those who don't ("naïfs") tend to overestimate their ability to avoid temptation with willpower alone. Those who do ("sophisticates") are better positioned to make change in their lives.

CHAPTER 4

Forgetfulness

I n a typical year in the United States, hundreds of thousands of
people are hospitalized with the flu and tens of thousands die.
Those are already alarming numbers, but in 2009, with both swine
flu *and* the seasonal flu spreading rapidly around the world, it was
looking to be an unusually bad year (though we'd eventually face a
far deadlier situation in 2020 with the COVID-19 pandemic).

That September, I was a newly minted professor eager to help
address this public health threat, and I agreed to fly to Nashville to
join a panel discussion on how to improve employee health and wellness at a Fortune 500 company. It was there that I met Prashant
Srivastava, the cofounder of Evive Health, who was also on the
panel. At the time, Prashant was working with companies across the
country to convince more of their employees to get vaccinated for
influenza.*

---

*A fairly effective swine flu vaccine was developed and offered along with the regular
seasonal flu vaccine in the fall of 2009 (M. R. Griffin et al., "Effectiveness of Non-
Adjuvanted Pandemic Influenza A Vaccines for Preventing Pandemic Influenza Acute

For years, Prashant had worked in the health care industry and watched in dismay as vast numbers of Americans failed to take advantage of all kinds of preventative care (such as getting a flu shot), even when it was free. Frustrated by this pattern, which struck him as eminently fixable, he cofounded Evive to try to change it. Evive works with companies to better communicate with their employees about when and how to take advantage of health benefits that too many never touch.

With the swine flu outbreak in full swing, Prashant's mission felt even more important than usual. But Evive had a problem. In the past, even when Evive's clients offered free flu shots at work, and even when Evive sent these employees personalized reminders about when and where to get their vaccination, only about 30 percent of employees followed through. While the swine flu epidemic led more people to *say* they'd get a flu shot in 2009, Prashant was doubtful. He'd seen people promise to get vaccinations and then drop the ball too many times. When I met him in Nashville, he told me he was stumped about what more to do. How could the company move the needle further?

Prashant's problem actually sounded extremely familiar to me. While I waited for my flight back home in the Nashville airport and grabbed a bite of barbecue (because there are some temptations I don't try to resist), I started pondering why and how I could help.

Respiratory Illness Visits in 4 U.S. Communities," *PLoS ONE* 6, no. 8 [2011]: e23085, DOI:10.1371/journal.pone.0023085).

VOTER FLAKE OUT

Roughly six months ahead of the 2008 U.S. presidential election, the Dow Jones Industrial Average had fallen 20 percent from its previous year's high, and the country's economy was in a tailspin by late September. The looming financial crisis was the great unknown factor in the coming election, but another key variable was that for the first time since 1952 neither party's nominee was an incumbent or the incumbent vice president. After a brutal primary season, Democratic nominee, Barack Obama, and Republican nominee, John McCain, were neck and neck in the polls.

As is the case in any close election, voter turnout had the potential to make or break the outcome of this high-stakes nail-biter. Thanks to the peculiar rules of the U.S. Electoral College, presidential elections can come down to thousands or even hundreds of votes in one or two states, as we learned from watching Al Gore lose to George W. Bush in 2000 by the narrowest of imaginable margins in Florida. Yet fewer than 60 percent of eligible U.S. voters typically turn up at the polls, which means that narrow victories do not necessarily reflect the will of the people.

Disturbed by these statistics and eager to take action to fix the problem, one of my closest friends in graduate school, Todd Rogers, was spending most of his waking hours leading up to the '08 election worrying about voter turnout. Now a decorated professor at the Harvard Kennedy School of Government, Todd was one of my "littermates" as a PhD student, which means we shared a dissertation adviser and were essentially intellectual siblings. He and I sat in matching cubicles in the same hallway for three years in graduate school, drank coffee together most mornings, and poked our heads in on one another at all hours to ask for help with everything from statistical modeling to relationships.

As we headed into the 2008 U.S. presidential primaries, I looked on as one particularly big puzzle began to obsess Todd. He had learned that huge numbers of registered voters say they plan to vote but then inevitably fail to show up at the polls. In fact, in one election he carefully studied, Todd and his collaborator Masahiko Aida discovered that 54 percent of registered voters who told pollsters they intended to vote "flaked out" (Todd and Masahiko's words), as measured by actual voter turnout records.

Todd wondered why so few registered voters followed through on their intentions. He recognized that getting even a small portion of these would-be voters to the polls in the upcoming U.S. election was an opportunity to improve the democratic process, and it seemed like particularly low-hanging fruit. These were people who were already registered to vote and had told pollsters they planned to turn out. They didn't need convincing that political participation was worthwhile. For some unknown reason, they just weren't making it to the polls.

In the Nashville airport in 2009, as I contemplated why so many Americans said they intended to get flu shots but failed to follow through, I realized why Prashant's struggle felt so familiar. I had seen Todd wrestle with the very same questions when he was studying voter flake out.

FORGETTING

Although I'd often heard Todd lament the challenge of countering voter flake out in grad school, I knew little about the origins of the problem. So I gave him a call. And the first thing he pointed out was that flake out is incredibly common. Flake out doesn't just prevent voters from turning up at the polls and employees from getting flu shots. It also prevents parents from regularly reading to their children, bosses from properly mentoring their subordinates, and the vast majority of Americans from sticking with their New Year's resolutions. In fact, evidence suggests that, surprisingly, our intentions are only loosely predictive of our behaviors.

Todd explained that his time spent learning everything he could about flake out from voter surveys, academic research, and introspection had taught him that it has a few particularly common causes. Good old laziness and inattention are a couple of them. But perhaps the biggest, most surprising, and easiest-to-overcome reason for flake out is that people simply forget. Todd was stunned to discover that "I forgot" is the most common explanation would-be voters offer for their failure to show up at the polls.

Forgetting might sound like a flimsy, made-up excuse for not getting around to something because you just don't care enough to make the effort, but even people who take voting very seriously can fall prey to the forgetfulness trap. Not long ago, a friend of mine who lives in Connecticut forgot to vote in an off-cycle election, even though she'd promised a candidate for local office that he had her support and she really wanted to stand by her pledge (commitments mean a lot to people, as you'll recall). She'd scheduled a work trip to

New York City on Election Day and meant to visit the polls before heading into Manhattan. But in the morning rush, voting simply slipped her mind. By the time she realized her mistake, she was already on a New York–bound train and wouldn't be back home in time to head to the polls. Though she told me she realized the election wasn't decided by one vote, she felt terrible anyway.

As this story illustrates, forgetfulness isn't always a made-up excuse. It's a more serious and common culprit for follow-through failures than you might think. According to one recent study, the average adult forgets three things each day, ranging from pin numbers to chores to wedding anniversaries. We're so forgetful, in part, because it's difficult for information to stick in our brains, especially if we've only thought about it once or twice. The German psychologist Hermann Ebbinghaus demonstrated how quickly humans forget in a classic study published in 1885. He attempted to memorize different sets of nonsense syllables and then tested his recollection at varying time intervals. With data from this experiment on his own memory, Hermann estimated that forgetting follows a roughly exponential decay function. We forget nearly half of the information we've learned within twenty minutes. After twenty-four hours, about 70 percent of it is gone, and a month later, we're looking at losses of approximately 80 percent. This basic pattern has also been replicated in more recent studies using similar experimental procedures.

Naturally, forgetting is more common the more we attempt to juggle, and the number of tasks and stimuli the average person has to keep track of these days is staggering. Take my schedule as an example. In the morning, I have to remember to shower, brush my teeth, get dressed, put on makeup, eat breakfast, dress my four-year-old for school, pack his lunch, snack, and water bottle in his backpack, brush his teeth, give him his asthma medicine, put on his sunblock, get him out the door with his grandparents, and pack my own purse (making sure not to forget my phone or, on a rainy day, my umbrella). And that's all before I head out the door to work. There's not a lot of room to think deeply about anything that isn't part of my routine or on my calendar, and as a result, I almost always forget something. Whether it's scheduling a dental checkup, voting, texting a friend a birthday message, or even recalling where I put my keys, you can be sure I'll drop a ball (or several) every day of the week.

Sometimes I even forget things that are *on* my calendar. Once, I missed an early morning breakfast meeting with a colleague who was in from out of town even though he'd confirmed two days ahead of time and I'd put it on my schedule. I just went about my regular morning routine without checking my calendar, since I never have meetings before 9:00 A.M. I didn't have the faintest idea that I'd spaced until I saw an email asking "Did one of us goof?" half an hour after our planned get-together. It was mortifying!

One obvious way to prevent this kind of mistake is to create reminder systems. And research has shown that reminders can help (so companies such as Evive are arguably doing a lot of good). Reminding people—by mail, telephone, or in person—to get immunizations, for instance, reduces flake out by an average of 8 percentage points. Similarly, in low-turnout elections, reminders sent by mail a little more than a week ahead of time can increase turnout among registered voters by as much as 6 percent. Reminders can also help people follow through when it comes to saving money. In a series of studies run with banks in Bolivia, Peru, and the Philippines, the very economist I stood up for breakfast (sorry again, Dean!) and a team of collaborators showed that sending monthly text messages or letters reminding customers to make savings deposits increased savings balances by roughly 6 percent.

But useful as they are, reminders unfortunately have serious limitations. One of Todd's favorite studies about reminders, which he described when filling me in on the flake out problem, illustrates this nicely.

The study, run in 2004 by John Austin, Sigurdur Sigurdsson, and Yonata Rubin at a large hotel and casino, involved reminding drivers to buckle up.* Four hundred and thirty-three patrons who had taken advantage of the hotel's valet parking services participated in the experiment, although they didn't know their behavior was being studied. Each patron was randomly assigned to one of three different experimental conditions, which determined what happened to them when they came to claim their valeted car.

Some patrons experienced business as usual. They gave their ticket to an attendant in the hotel's valet parking area, waited for their car to be pulled around, and then drove off. Another group was prompted by the parking attendant to "Be safe, remember to fasten your seat belt!" upon handing over their claim ticket. For the final group, the parking attendant delivered the same reminder, but not until the driver was entering her vehicle.

The difference between the two reminders tested in this study was quite subtle. All of the drivers heard the same reminder before pulling out of the valet lot. The only difference was that some heard it an average of four minutes and fifty seconds before stepping into their

---

*We're left to guess which casino was the site of this experiment, but one of the study's authors was an analyst at Caesars Entertainment, so that provides a clue.

cars (the typical time it took valets to retrieve automobiles), while others heard it just as they entered their vehicles. Big deal, right?

Well, it turned out to be a *huge* deal.

Trained student observers surreptitiously tracked which drivers in the study actually buckled up. Somewhat surprisingly, given how well reminders generally work, there wasn't a significant difference in seat belt use between drivers who were reminded to buckle up a few minutes before their car was pulled around and drivers who heard no reminder at all. About 55 percent of drivers buckled up in both cases.*

The only group that differed substantially was the one that was reminded to buckle up *right* as they stepped into their cars. Eighty percent of these patrons strapped on their seat belts.

That's a whopping 25 percentage point increase in an incredibly important safety behavior, driven only by a subtle change in the timing of a reminder. I harp on the importance of this study whenever I teach my students about combatting forgetting. This finding makes it clear: Reminders work far, far better when we can act on them immediately.

Just think of the reminder email my colleague sent me two days before our breakfast meeting—it didn't help a bit at 7:00 A.M. on the day of our scheduled rendezvous when I was going about my usual morning routine. And my friend in Connecticut who forgot to vote got many reminders—they just didn't come on the morning of the election as she was hurriedly preparing to catch a train to New York City.

You've probably experienced this problem, too. Consider how

---

*It's worth noting that the study was small, so it wasn't well designed to measure subtle changes in behavior.

rarely it helps to have your spouse or roommate remind you, in the morning, to pick something up after work. Will you really still hear that voice in your head after a busy day at the office? Unless the conversation prompts you to create another, more timely reminder on your calendar or initiates such a lengthy discussion that the to-do item is burned into your brain, a morning reminder about an afternoon activity is rarely of much use. The seat belt study shows that *even a five-minute delay* between a reminder to buckle up and the chance to strap in was enough for drivers to forget what they were meant to do when they entered their vehicles. Hermann Ebbinghaus's exponential forgetting curve means we need to get the timing right.

When Todd shared these findings with me, he admitted that upon first learning about them, he had despaired. How could he effectively combat forgetting if he couldn't be the metaphorical valet, whispering in voters' ears to go to the polls right as they were leaving home or work?

CUE-BASED PLANNING

In his search for an answer, Todd encountered one particularly intriguing study conducted in the 1990s at the University of Munich right before the school's Christmas break. The study's authors asked roughly one hundred students to name a difficult goal they hoped to achieve during their time away from the university. The students shared all kinds of objectives, ranging from "write a term paper" to "find a new apartment" to "settle a conflict with my boyfriend."

Christmas is a magical time of year in Munich, a city nestled at the foot of the snowy Bavarian Alps and dotted with Christmas markets during the holidays. Distractions were sure to lead some students astray, and the researchers knew it. But they were curious to see who would manage to achieve their goals, and why.

Shortly after Christmas, the students were asked to report on what they'd accomplished. And a remarkable pattern emerged. Students who had approached their goals in the typical way had a measly 22 percent success rate, while those who had made just a little tweak to the standard approach reported a whopping 62 percent success rate.

So what was the tweak?

It was something the study's author—renowned New York University psychology professor Peter Gollwitzer—calls forming an "implementation intention." This fancy term actually refers to a fairly straightforward strategy the group of students with the higher success rate used: making a plan for achieving a goal and linking it to a specific cue that will remind you to act. A cue can be something simple, such as a date and time (say, 3:00 P.M. on Tuesday), or more complex, such as passing a specific Dunkin' Donuts on the way to the office.

Often when we make plans, we don't focus on what will trigger us to act. Instead, we focus on what we intend to do. For instance, a typical plan to improve oral hygiene might be: "I'm going to start flossing more." Peter's work shows it's vital to link that intention with a cue, such as a specific time, place, or action. If you want to floss more regularly, a helpful tweak to your plan would be to say, "*Every night after brushing my teeth,* I'm going to floss."

Forming an implementation intention is as simple as filling in the blanks in the sentence "When ___ happens, I'll do ___." So "I plan to increase my monthly retirement savings" has a missing ingredient that lowers your chance of success, but "Whenever I get a raise, I'll increase my monthly retirement savings" is a more complete plan. Similarly, "I'm going to spend more time on my online master's" is too vague, while "On Tuesdays and Thursdays at 5:00 P.M., I'll spend an hour working on my online master's" is better. And "I'll walk to work more" isn't quite right, but "Anytime it's between thirty-five and eighty degrees Fahrenheit and isn't raining or snowing, I'll walk to work" does the trick.

In numerous survey studies, Peter has shown that simply asking people to form cue-based plans vastly increases their likelihood of goal achievement. Further, the more easily a person can detect the cue needed to enact their plan (thanks to details and specificity), the better. So a plan to get in shape, like "Every Tuesday and Thursday right after work I'll exercise, and I'll take the number 17 bus to the YMCA on Main Street where I'll work out for thirty minutes on the elliptical" is a lot more helpful than "I'll exercise more" or even "On Tuesdays and Thursdays I'll go to the gym."

When Todd discovered Peter's research in the lead-up to the 2008 election, he thought he'd found a low-cost, easy-to-deploy way to help combat voter flake out. And as he dug into the literature on implementation intentions, Todd unpacked everything that was known about why cue-based plans help people.

First, as he later explained to me, making such detailed plans requires some time and effort. And the more time and effort we put into thinking about something, the deeper it gets lodged in our memories. In fact, this is one of the key findings that came out of Hermann Ebbinghaus's classic research on forgetting in the 1880s. The more we engage with information, the longer it's recalled. This finding has been replicated many times and helps explain why so many of us are encouraged to memorize material by using flash cards, which make it easy to repeatedly engage with the information we hope to learn.

But cues alone also turn out to be closely linked with human recall. Think of the way hearing an old song (an auditory cue) can bring back a specific memory. Anytime I hear "When I'm Sixty-Four" by the Beatles I remember my wedding, because it played during the recessional. And the 1993 hit song "The Sign" by Ace of Base makes me think of a Christmas I spent with a cousin in Texas singing its catchy refrain over and over again. You probably have some funny examples, too.

When memories come flooding back, it's because they're stored and retrieved through all kinds of cues: sights, sounds, smells, tastes, and even textures. In perhaps the most famous depiction of the power of taste to evoke memories, the protagonist of Marcel Proust's novel *In Search of Lost Time* bites into a madeleine cookie, which unleashes a flood of childhood recollections. In the words of the narrator, "Suddenly the memory returns" of summer Sundays spent with his aunt as a child in the country, where he ate the very same delicious treats.

The power that cues have to trigger memories means that linking a plan (such as flossing) with a cue you expect to encounter (such as your nightly tooth-brushing ritual) makes it far more likely that you'll remember the plan. The cue will retrieve the memory of what you're supposed to do.

No matter what type of cue you use, Peter Gollwitzer's research shows that cue-based action plans are a remarkable salve for the forgetting problem.

THE BEST KINDS OF CUES

One sunny morning in April, Todd launched an experiment to see if there might be a simple way to make cues even more useful (and he brought me in on the fun). He hired several research assistants to stand outside a popular café in Harvard Square on a busy Tuesday morning and offer hundreds of customers coupons for 1 dollar off their purchase the following Thursday. The research assistants were helping me and Todd evaluate a new way to combat forgetting. As they handed out coupons, they also delivered instructions. Some customers received an ordinary cue to jog their memory—they were handed a picture of the café's cash register and advised to remember to redeem their coupon when they saw it, as usual, at checkout.

But other customers in our study got a more distinctive prompt—one we suspected would be more effective. They were given a picture of the same cash register, but with a stuffed, three-eyed alien from *Toy Story* sitting in front of it and advised to remember to redeem their 1 dollar off when they saw the alien.

When that Thursday rolled around and our coupons could be redeemed, we placed the plush alien in front of the cash register where everyone could see it, as promised. But because we'd told only a subset of patrons to look out for it, it had a different meaning to different people. For some, it was a reminder to redeem their coupon. Everyone else just wondered why the café's usually tasteful décor had been hijacked.

Todd and I had a theory that the more distinctive the cue, the more effective it would be at driving recall, and we turned out to be right. Customers who were instructed to look out for the stuffed alien were 36 percent more likely than the others to remember to redeem their 1 dollar off.

This study and a series of follow-up experiments taught us that while any cue is better than no cue, it's best to rely on cues that are out of the ordinary. Encountering something odd in your path (like a toy alien) captures your attention, which is, after all, a limited resource.

This research actually relates to ancient wisdom on committing things to memory. A manuscript written in the 80s BC called *Rhetorica ad Herennium* first introduced a now popular idea that to commit things to memory, we can link them with vivid scenes or objects. This is the origin of "memory palaces." To memorize information using a memory palace, you associate each item you hope to recall with scenes or places you know well. For instance, you might use your house (your "palace") to commit a list to memory by imagining a walk through it and festooning each room you encounter with vivid imagery evoking items on your list. If you need to remember a long series of actions (say, picking up a prescription, dropping off muffins at a bake sale, mailing a letter, and so on), you might imagine pill bottles lining your entryway, muffins covering your kitchen, and letters piled in your bedroom. Then when it's time to recall the day's to-dos, you could close your eyes, make your way through your imagined house (filled with odd decorations) and recall what was in each room to trigger your memory. Research shows that using this technique to memorize a twelve-item shopping list doubles the number of people who can recall at least eleven of twelve items.

Useful mnemonic devices like these can also be auditory. When I was taught about the subclassification of animals first into *k*ingdom, then *p*hylum, then *c*lass, then *o*rder, then *f*amily, then *g*enus, and finally, species, I learned the phrase "*Kings Play Chess on Fine Green Silk.*" The first letter of each word cues a memory of one of these categories and reminds me of their proper order.

When creating cue-based plans, it's wise to keep these lessons in mind. The more vivid, catchy, and thus memorable the cue, the more likely it is to do its job and help us recall our plans.

INCREASING VOTER TURNOUT

Every year leading up to Election Day, campaign volunteers and hired hands contact millions of registered voters by phone, reminding them to cast ballots at their local polling stations. This process unfolds in democracies all around the world from the U.S. to the U.K., from Canada to India, and from Norway to Australia. If you're a registered voter living in a democracy, you've surely gotten at least one of these carefully scripted calls, during which you were implored to make it to the polls (probably much to your annoyance). Maybe the call was enough to set you in motion, but more likely, it wasn't critical to your decision about whether or not to vote.

By mid-2008, Todd was confident from all he'd learned about voter flake out that these calls could be drastically improved and saw them as a golden opportunity. He suspected they would be a perfect vehicle for testing new ways to motivate more voters to show up at the polls. And he had a good feeling about Peter Gollwitzer's studies suggesting that cue-based plans can solve follow-through problems. He just needed to confirm that Peter's ideas could be taken out of the psychology laboratory and into the world of politics. With the 2008 election fast approaching, Todd decided it was high time to put them to the test.

After consulting carefully with Peter, Todd and his collaborator David Nickerson developed a voter call script with a special new feature. Instead of simply urging registered voters to show up on Election Day as usual, Todd's new script also prompted voters to describe specifically how and when they would get to the polls. Todd and I now call this a "planning prompt."

Todd and David designed their script so a professional call center could deliver it to tens of thousands of registered voters in the three days leading up to a major U.S. primary. First, callers would ask registered voters if they planned to vote. If the reply was yes, they would follow up with three questions: (1) "What time do you expect you'll head to the polls?" (2) "Where do you expect you'll be coming from?" and (3) "What do you think you'll be doing before you head out?" These questions were selected to ensure voters had carefully considered the cues (time, location, and activity) that would remind them it was time to vote.

In total, in their 2008 test of planning prompts, Todd and David randomized nearly forty thousand registered voters to either hear a standard get-out-the-vote call script (which simply asked people if they intended to vote and exhorted them to do so) or a script with those three extra questions, which prompted the formation of a voting plan.

Naturally, when Todd analyzed the voter turnout rolls, he was hoping to see a big effect—the kind that might really boost political participation in democracies around the world. And his wish came true: among registered voters who picked up the phone, hearing a planning prompt increased voter turnout by 9 percent. Todd knew he had a game changer on his hands.

But there was something even more interesting in Todd's data. He discovered that these planning prompts mattered a lot more to some people than to others.

Consider two types of registered voters. Some of us live in "multi-voter households" with family or friends who've also registered to vote. Others live alone or with roommates who aren't eligible to participate in elections, maybe because they're too young or because they've never registered to vote, or perhaps because they aren't U.S. citizens. These voters live in "single-voter households."

Todd could tell if the eligible voters in his study lived in multi-voter or single-voter households, and he saw a big difference between the two groups. Prompting registered voters to make a voting plan was *twice* as effective for those in single-voter households as it was for those in multi-voter households. When asked about their voting plans over the phone, people in single-voter households were substantially less likely than others to already know what time they would vote, where they would be coming from, and what they would be doing before voting.

And it didn't take much sleuthing to figure out why: there was something fundamentally different about what was happening *organically* in the homes of different types of voters before they got a call encouraging them to make a voting plan.

Voters in multi-voter households were naturally having conversations with their family, friends, and roommates to coordinate their voting plans. For instance, my husband and I usually go to the polling station around the corner from our house together on Election Day, and we usually talk through the timing beforehand, plotting whether it will be better to go before or after work depending on what else we have on the calendar. But voters in single-voter households are, naturally, far less likely to have those kinds of conversations. And as a result, Todd found that many fewer of them had well-thought-out voting plans when they got a call prompting them to come up with one. So it's no wonder that being asked to plan had a much bigger impact on people in single-voter homes—the exercise was more useful because they hadn't yet figured out the cues that would help them remember to turn out at the polls.

When Todd put this all together, he was thrilled. He knew he could use these new insights about voters to help more people follow through on their intentions to participate in the political process.* He also suspected, correctly, that the discoveries he'd made could help solve a far wider set of flake out problems in other contexts.

BOOSTING VACCINATIONS

Enthusiastic as I was to learn of Todd's successes with voter mobilization when we caught up on the details after my trip to Nashville, I worried a lot about whether or not his findings were universal. I hoped that a remix of Todd's recipe could help Prashant Srivastava and Evive increase flu vaccination rates, but I saw a few big reasons why it might not translate. For one thing, though there are important commonalities between voting and getting a flu shot (notably, they're

---

*In 2008, Todd cofounded a nonprofit called the Analyst Institute that uses behavioral science toward this end. If you're interested in learning more, Sasha Issenberg's book *The Victory Lab: The Secret Science of Winning Campaigns* (Broadway Books, 2012) chronicles the Analyst Institute's early history.

both things that people think they should do but often don't), there are also some crucial differences, ranging from a fear of side effects and pain to the degree of self-interest involved (flu shots protect you from illness, but voting typically has less tangible consequences).

More important, Todd had been able to reach registered voters by phone, and Evive communicated with its customers only via the U.S. Postal Service. Would prompting people to make plans be as effective by snail mail? It seemed possible, but hardly a sure thing. When someone is talking you through a series of planning questions, you face significant social pressure to make a plan. Not responding is rude. But if you were asked similar questions in a letter and expected to make plans in private without any way to reply, there is less chance that you would bother.

On top of that, it wasn't totally clear whether Todd's planning prompts actually combatted *forgetting* or if they addressed other reasons for flake out. Maybe because would-be voters were telling another person about how they planned to vote, answering questions from Todd's team by phone felt like making a pledge, creating a soft commitment not to flake out. As we saw in the previous chapter, we're psychologically wired to find it uncomfortable to say one thing and do another (cognitive dissonance), which is why pledges can help change our behavior. Taking the same approach in a flu shot mailing might not work, because we wouldn't be asking people to commit to another person.

Still, adapting these ideas to tackle the flu shot flake out problem seemed worth a try. So I worked with a team of economists* to convince Evive to make a small addition to a standard reminder letter.

---

*John Beshears, James Choi, David Laibson, and Brigitte Madrian.

Recipients would be encouraged to write down the date and time when they planned to get their flu shot at their free workplace clinic.*

It's worth noting here that these letters weren't inviting people to schedule flu shot appointments. That often confuses audiences when I present this study. The letters provided no mail-back address and no way for the recipients to convey their flu shot plan to Evive or their employer. We simply hoped that a prompt to think through a concrete plan with a time trigger could help them follow through on getting an important vaccination by combatting forgetting.

Prashant was hopeful, too. If simple changes like this to the company's reminder forms could make a difference without costing Evive a dime, it would be a huge boon.

So when we tested our letters experimentally at a large midwestern company with dozens of offices and saw substantive changes in vaccination rates, everyone celebrated. Much to our delight, merely prompting people to write down a plan in the privacy of their home led to a 13 percent increase in vaccinations, though no one from Evive ever heard or saw these plans.† Many more people than usual in our study followed through to get an immunization they wanted, lowering their risk of a nasty illness.

Interestingly though, like Todd, we found that the prompts were much more helpful in some contexts than others. Offices that held

---

*The callout boxes first noted that many people find making a flu shot plan helpful, and then we encouraged people to write down their own plan on the form. We left blanks on the mailing where people could jot down the day of the week, date, and time when they planned to get a shot and even included a picture of a pencil to convey that we were really asking recipients to write down a plan.

†When we looked not only at who got vaccinated at workplace flu shot clinics but also at flu shot insurance claims overall (including trips to the doctor's office or a local pharmacy to get vaccinated), the effects were even slightly bigger—all at no added cost to Evive.

one-day-only clinics—so that remembering to show up that day was a make-or-break affair—benefited enormously, while offices with multi-day clinics didn't benefit much at all.

In a follow-up study with Evive, my team showed that the same kinds of planning prompts that boosted flu shot follow-through also helped patients overdue for a colonoscopy get their acts together, increasing the fraction who received life-saving screenings by 15 percent. Here, the benefits of a prompt to plan were biggest for the very populations whom we suspected were most likely to struggle with remembering to get a colonoscopy—older adults, parents, those with less insurance coverage, and people who had ignored previous reminders.

Together, all of this research on planning prompts has convinced me that encouraging people to make a plan, whether over the phone or in the privacy of their own homes, is an underappreciated way to combat flaking out. Naturally, thinking through the where and when of anything I want to get done is now a strategy that I rely on constantly in both my personal and professional life. I use it to make sure I get vaccinated, pay bills, exercise, and check in with students. And I use it to help other people, too. When my friend Jason told me he'd been meaning to write a letter of gratitude to a former mentor and kept flaking out, I asked him the date and time when he would write it, how he would write it (email or snail mail?), and if his plan was entered in his calendar. Then I sent him a timely reminder. Not only did Jason's mentor get a letter of gratitude that week; I got one, too.

AN ADDED BONUS:
BREAKING THINGS DOWN

In June 2019, I spent an exciting but exhausting thirty-six hours in London with my colleague Angela Duckworth, speaking at a variety of venues about our joint research. We were looking to generate excitement and spread the word about a scientific center we codirect that coordinates studies on behavior change. During one of our presentations, Lloyd Thomas, a managing partner at a London-based private equity and venture capital firm, raised his hand. Lloyd declared himself a behavioral science junkie. He'd read all the books and listened to all the podcasts, and now he needed to know one thing: Which of the many behavioral insights he'd learned about was most important to helping him achieve his goals?

Angela didn't hesitate before giving her answer—to her, it was blindingly obvious: cue-based plans. Forming these kinds of plans most effectively sets you up for success, she told him. It's the best insight behavioral science has to offer on this topic.

I'm not sure how Lloyd felt about that reply, but I was a little surprised. To be totally honest, though I've always thought planning was important, I've never thought it was among the most inspired strategies I'd studied. If pressed, I might have picked making goal pursuit fun or using a commitment device.

So I pushed Angela to elaborate on her answer to Lloyd's question. And I have to admit, what she said made a lot of sense. Angela pointed out that in addition to reducing forgetting and short-circuiting the need to think about what you'll do in the moment, planning forces you to break big goals into bite-size chunks. This turns out to be really important to making progress on ambitious projects (as I explained in the previous chapter). Just imagine how hopeless it would have been for John F. Kennedy to declare in 1962 that Americans would go to the moon by the end of the decade if teams of NASA engineers hadn't broken that enormous goal into a series of subgoals with detailed plans for how each would be accomplished. Similarly, when you have a big goal you hope to achieve, such as "earn a promotion in the next year," planning forces you to do the critical work of breaking it down. Planning for how to earn a promotion might lead you to recognize that you'll need to better communicate with your boss in weekly meetings, advocate for recognition of your work, and spend Tuesday and Thursday evenings studying to complete your online degree. Without this kind of planning, which forces you to do the critical work of understanding what achieving your goal actually entails, your goal will likely remain elusive. If you have a simple goal, such as voting in the next election, ensuring that you remember to follow through is all you need to do. But for *complex* goals, such as learning a foreign language, planning involves not just remembering to follow through, but also breaking your goal down into smaller, more concrete components.

Forming cue-based plans is, of course, something you can do yourself (if, like Lloyd, you're working on personal goals). But it's also something a good manager, company, policy maker, or friend can prompt you to do, as exemplified by Evive Health's flu shot reminders and Todd's get-out-the-vote efforts. And a particularly nice thing about prompting *other* people to make plans is that you don't have to twist any arms.

If someone isn't interested in following through in the first place, forming a cue-based plan won't change that. You can tell me all day long to make cue-based plans to get an eyebrow piercing or go bungee jumping, but it will have no effect on me because I'm not interested in doing either. Plans don't change minds—they only help us remember to do the things we already want to do. So they're a nice, noncoercive way you can help other people achieve their own goals.

At the end of our London trip, after Angela and I had debated the issue for a while, she convinced me: cue-based planning belongs at the top of any list of behavioral science insights that can spur goal achievement.

That said, there is one important caveat.

Research has shown that you can overdo it on cue-based planning. Having too many plans can overwhelm us. If we form multiple cue-based plans for competing goals (to exercise more and to learn a foreign language and to get a promotion and to renovate the kitchen), we're forced to face the fact that doing everything required to succeed will be really tough. And this leads our commitment to dwindle, making it harder to achieve even one of our goals.

Just think of all the steps you have to lay out to achieve a single goal like getting that promotion. Then think about tripling or even quadrupling your to-do list as you form plans for all your other goals, too. It's a little mind-boggling, not to mention demoralizing. So it's best to be choosy about which goals you'll focus on at a given time and plan carefully to achieve just one or two. You might choose a single top priority this month (say, exercising four times a week) and plan for it. Then next month, you can turn to whatever is second on your list.

Another potential complication with cue-based planning is that what you need to remember to do can be so complex that a simple

plan to act won't suffice. In these cases, research shows that a formal checklist can work wonders. As Atul Gawande explained in his
book *The Checklist Manifesto*, when surgeons rely on simple safety
checklists for a procedure rather than on their memories of what
steps are necessary, it saves lives, cutting complications and mortality rates by an estimated 35 to 45 percent. And checklists don't just
help with safety. A recent experiment demonstrated that providing
checklists to auto mechanics vastly increased their productivity and
revenues.

DO IT YOURSELF

Happily, cue-based plans have become more and more popular.
Thanks to resounding evidence from Todd's research that they boost
turnout, planning prompts have become a staple of get-out-the-vote
efforts worldwide. While most of us are a little disgruntled when a
stranger knocks on our door, Todd told me that he now lights up
when a political canvasser comes to his house. "I hear her script and
I'm eager, really happy," he confessed somewhat bashfully. After
enthusiastically answering canvassers' planning questions, he always asks to snap a photo of their scripts, which are based on his
work.

Similarly, since the first study Evive and I did together in 2009,
the company has made planning prompts a staple of its communications strategy. And while the company was a ten-person start-up
with a few major clients when I first met Prashant, it now boasts
three hundred employees and regularly messages roughly five million

Americans about how to plan and make better health decisions. Not only that, but after the publication of our Evive experiments, many other organizations began using the same insight with great results. From banks prompting plans for loan repayment to governments prompting plans for water conservation and vaccination, nudges to think carefully about the when and where of follow-through are now widespread.

The fact is that there are many things we routinely forget to do in spite of having good intentions. Voting and getting vaccinated are just the tip of the proverbial iceberg. But setting timely reminders and planning with vivid cues are valuable tools to help you combat your own tendency to flake out. And the great thing about cue-based planning is that you don't need a benevolent organization such as Evive or a savvy manager or friend to coach you through it. When you have a goal that you're afraid you might flake out on, you can create cue-based plans on your own now that you know the formula.

Just remember to consider the how, when, and where: How will you do it? When will you do it? Where will you do it? Be strategic about the cues you select—if you can, choose cues that are out of the ordinary. When I'm lying in bed at night and realize I have an important task to remember the next day, I try to think of something atypical that I'll encounter in the morning (maybe the Lego structure my son just built and left in our living room). That becomes the cue I use when I form a plan to follow-through. And if you can arrange to schedule a reminder that will appear at the *very* moment when you should act, do so posthaste. Finally, if your cue-based plans start to get complicated, consider developing a checklist.

———————— Chapter Takeaways ————————

- Sometimes we flake out and fail to follow through on our intentions. Flake out has many causes, including laziness, distraction, and forgetting. Forgetting may be the easiest of these obstacles to overcome.

- Timely reminders, which prompt you to do something *right* before you're meant to do it, can effectively combat forgetting. Reminders that aren't as timely have far smaller benefits.

- Forming cue-based plans is another way to combat forgetting. These plans link a plan of action with a cue and take the form "When ___ happens, I'll do ___." Cues can be anything that triggers your memory, from a specific time or location to an object you expect to encounter. An example of a cue-based plan is, "Whenever I get a raise, I'll increase my monthly retirement savings contribution."

- The more distinctive the cue, the more likely it is to trigger recall.

- Prompting people to form cue-based plans is particularly useful when they are unlikely to have already formed plans and when forgetting is a make-or-break affair (as is the case with voting on Election Day).

- Planning also has other benefits: It helps you break your goals into bite-size chunks, relieves you of the need to think about what you'll do in the moment, and acts like a pledge to yourself, thereby increasing your commitment to your goal.

• If you form too many cue-based plans at once, you may be discouraged and your commitment may dwindle. So be choosy about which goals you'll plan for at any given time.

• When plans get too complex to remember easily, rely on checklists.

CHAPTER 5

Laziness

W hat in the world happened?" Steve Honeywell wondered. Steve worked as an analyst at the University of
Pennsylvania's massive health system, and one day in
the fall of 2014 he couldn't make heads or tails of a graph he'd just
created. According to his data, a persistent problem that had been
costing the health system and its patients roughly 15 million dollars
per year had disappeared overnight. This was not normal.

So he started putting out feelers. "Did anything big change last
month at the hospital? Were new best practices rolled out or something?" he asked his boss. "Could someone check?"

I first heard the story of Steve's baffling discovery when I invited
Mitesh Patel, a talented physician and Wharton alumnus, to guest
lecture in my MBA class. Mitesh runs a group at the University of
Pennsylvania's health system that, rumor had it, was accomplishing
great things with behavioral science. And after he'd finished sharing
his first slide, it was clear that these rumors were true.

At the start of my class, Mitesh told us about Steve Honeywell's miraculous discovery and why it mattered. Up until 2014, Penn's health system had been incurring fines from its largest insurer for its doctors' prescription practices. Much to the chagrin of Penn Medicine's leaders, the medical staff habitually prescribed brand-name medications such as Lipitor and Viagra instead of cheaper but chemically identical generic drugs.

This might not sound like a big deal, but patients were spending millions of extra dollars each year as a result. And insurers were paying a huge price as well, which led them to fine and complain to Penn Medicine. It was particularly frustrating because the problem seemed easy to fix. Doctors were badgered frequently to stop prescribing brand-name drugs and promised to reform, but too many didn't.

And then came the incredible change that Steve Honeywell discovered. Overnight, according to his data, Penn Medicine went from the worst health system in the region when it came to prescribing generic drugs to the best. Only 75 percent of the health system's prescriptions were generic in the month prior to Steve's startling analysis; now Penn's doctors were prescribing generic medicines 98 percent of the time. Bonuses and goodwill from insurers followed.

In my MBA class, Mitesh shared the secret behind the revolutionary change that had blown Steve's mind that day in 2014. It wasn't a fresh start or timely reminder that shifted the doctors' behavior. Instead, a tiny, costless system change was behind the miraculous improvement.

THE PATH OF LEAST RESISTANCE

To explain what went right at Penn Medicine, let's consider a barrier to change that I haven't yet mentioned in this book: laziness.

Laziness is widely viewed as a vice we should work hard to over-come. Countless stories from cultures all over the world—from "The Little Red Hen" to Aesop's fable "The Ant and the Grasshopper"—teach us that indolence ends in ruin and industriousness in prosperity.*

There's a lot of truth in that lesson, of course. The human tendency to take the path of least resistance—to be passive and go with the flow—has downsides. It's a major reason behavior change can be so hard. When you resolve to spend your evenings earning an online degree instead of binge-watching Netflix, or to start cooking fresh meals instead of ordering takeout, your laziness and comfort with familiar patterns of behavior can work against you.

But laziness isn't always a vice. Instead of seeing our inherent lazi-ness as a bug, I regard it as a feature with many upsides. While it can unquestionably get in the way of behavior change, it also prevents us from wasting oodles of time and energy. As Herbert Simon, the 1978 Nobel laureate in economics, points out in his seminal book *Admin-istrative Behavior*, taking the path of least resistance is exactly what the world's best computer programs do when solving problems, in order to avoid using costly processing power. The best search algorithms, like the one that paid for Google's lavish campus in Mountain View, work fast and effectively because they take shortcuts rather than exploring every possible option. Humans have evolved to have the same knack

---

*In case you're unfamiliar with these classic tales, here's a quick summary. In the "The Ant and the Grasshopper," a carefree grasshopper chooses to spend his days singing and play-ing music while his friend the ant busily prepares grain stores for winter and (unsuccess-fully) admonishes the grasshopper to do the same. In the end, the grasshopper has nothing to eat when the cold arrives, while the ant is well fed. In "The Little Red Hen," a hen plants, harvests, and mills wheat, and then bakes it into bread, asking her friends for help throughout the process. Her friends all decline her pleas for aid; but when the time comes to feast, they're eager to partake. However, the hen gives her friends the same answer they had previously given her, leaving them hungry while she enjoys the fruits of her labor.

for efficiency. Because I'm lazy enough to call the first plumber with good reviews on Yelp when I need a toilet fixed, I don't waste time researching endless alternatives that might be marginally better. Because I'm happy to accept the factory settings on a new computer, I don't have to agonize over choices about screensavers or font sizes. And because I'm too lazy to rethink my morning routine, I don't have to ponder whether I should shower or brush my teeth first, what to have for breakfast, or what route to take to the office.

Laziness can be an asset. And not just when it comes to efficiency. When laziness is appropriately harnessed, it can actually help facilitate change. And that's exactly what happened at Penn Medicine.

SET IT AND FORGET IT

Penn Medicine's miraculous success rested squarely on people's tendency to take the path of least resistance. During a routine system upgrade, an IT consultant working on the software that Penn physicians used to send prescriptions to pharmacies made a small change to the user interface: he added a new checkbox to the system. From then on, unless a physician checked that box, whatever drug they prescribed would be sent to the pharmacy as a generic. Since doctors, like the rest of us, tend to be a little lazy, they only rarely checked the box: just 2 percent of the time. As a result, Penn's generic prescription rate shot up to 98 percent.

Behavioral scientists would describe what happened at Penn Medicine by saying the IT consultant changed the prescription system "default," or the outcome the system delivered if no one actively chose another option (such as the standard factory settings that come with a new computer). If defaults are set wisely, you'll still end up making the best decision even if you don't lift a finger—an opportunity most of us relish, thanks to our efficiency-loving operating systems.

For years at Penn Medicine, Mitesh and his colleagues had been lobbying to change the prescription interface to automatically order generics unless doctors opted out. But final approval was still pending. In the end, a lone IT developer, knowing that good defaults matter, took it upon himself to make the change when Penn Medicine's software system needed updating anyway. And *boom!*—millions of dollars were saved. This success was so colossal that Mitesh was given the green light to form a new Penn Medicine "Nudge Unit" to implement more deliberate system improvements grounded in behavioral science.

Nudging is a term bandied about a lot in the behavioral science community. Although there are many different ways to *nudge* behavior change, the term is often used as a synonym for setting good defaults because this type of nudge, which harnesses human laziness for good, has proven *so* valuable. For instance, a now extremely famous 2001 study proved that defaulting people into savings plans—making it necessary to opt out (rather than to opt in)—vastly increases saving for retirement.* Decades of additional research have now convincingly proven that setting defaults wisely is a great way to create big wins. By designing systems to produce the best possible outcome

---

*This study helped spur the 2006 U.S. Pension Protection Act, which awards tax breaks to employers who default their employees into 401(k) savings programs (Public Law 109–280 [2006]). Another famous study done in 2003 showed that in countries where citizens are organ donors by default (with an easy opt-out option), the fraction of registered donors is more than six times higher than in countries with the opposite default (Eric Johnson and Daniel Goldstein, "Do Defaults Save Lives?" *Science* 302, no. 5649 [November 2003]: 1338–39, DOI:10.1126/science.1091721).

when most of us, inevitably, fail to lift a finger, those familiar with the power of defaults have helped reduce the overprescription of opioids, limit children's soda consumption, boost flu vaccination rates, and raise tips on taxi rides, and that's just the beginning.*

Unfortunately, "set-it-and-forget-it" systems can't solve every behavior change problem. When you need to *take an action*, and particularly when you need to do it repeatedly, it's hard to rely on defaults. There's no default setting you can change that will ensure you exercise regularly, eat a healthy diet, ignore social media at work, or study for your exams. When we face repeated decisions, laziness is harder to tackle. You can certainly set wise defaults to encourage some of those regular decisions, such as keeping only healthy food in the fridge or setting *The New York Times* as your browser's homepage instead of Facebook. But what can you do about the rest? When inertia is working against you and a default switch can't be flipped, how can you engineer change?

HOW HABITS WORK

Stephen Kesting's heart raced as he desperately searched for his missing teammate inside the burning warehouse. In all his years as a firefighter, this was the biggest blaze he'd seen. Before the building went up in flames, it had housed boxes upon boxes of tissues, paper towels, and thousand-pound rolls of paper. Now, everything was kindling.

---

*Research shows that defaults can influence our behavior for other reasons as well. People assume the default is the recommended option, or the most popular option, and rejecting the default can often feel like a loss (Jon M. Jachimowicz et al., "When and Why Defaults Influence Decisions: A Meta-Analysis of Default Effects," *Behavioural Public Policy* 3, no. 2 [2019]: 159–86, DOI:10.1017/bpp.2018.43).

When Stephen's team arrived on the scene, the fire was already dangerously out of control. But just before he entered the building, things got worse: "Everything inside had fallen down like a row of dominoes," Stephen explained when he was a guest on my podcast. That would be scary enough under normal circumstances, but with a member of his crew unaccounted for inside the building, it was terrifying.

As Stephen's adrenaline spiked, his reflexes took over. That's a behavioral side effect of intense fear or excitement—a heavier reliance on your automatic systems and less deep thinking about each decision. There are obvious advantages to this. An emergency is generally no time to take out your calculator or start weighing pros and cons. You need to act quickly. But that also means it's critical to have good reflexes and habits.

Habits are the behaviors and routines we've repeated, consciously or subconsciously, so many times that they've become automatic. They are essentially our brain's default setting: the responses we enact without conscious processing. Neuroscience research shows that as habits develop, we rely less and less on the parts of our brain that are used for reasoning (the prefrontal cortex) and more and more on the parts that are responsible for action and motor control (the basal ganglia and cerebellum).*

Because firefighters and other first responders need to be able to do the right thing without much deliberate thinking, they spend enormous amounts of time practicing and drilling for emergencies,

---

*As Charles Darwin pointed out in his classic work *On the Origin of Species*, the key distinction between instincts and habits is their source: we're born with instincts but habits are learned (Charles Darwin and Leonard Kebler, *On the Origin of Species by Means of Natural Selection, or, The Preservation of Favoured Races in the Struggle for Life* [London: J. Murray, 1859]).

building muscle memory and developing routines that turn smart judgments into gut reactions. At the fire academy and on the job, they drill and drill to cut down the time and thought it takes to put on their heavy gear and load their trucks when the fire alarm goes off. They practice search-and-rescue skills, learn how to pull a hose line, and rehearse what to do if an oxygen mask fails.

As Stephen searched for his missing teammate in that terrifying warehouse fire, he relied on the habits he'd honed through practice. He called out, "Hello! Hello! Fire department! Anyone here?" just as he'd been trained to do. But that was the easy part. "The hard part," he explained, "is to teach people to shut up afterward and create a moment of silence . . . so you can look and listen and hopefully see or hear something." Your natural instinct in that kind of situation is to keep yelling, which prevents you from searching effectively.

Thankfully, Stephen and his team had practiced that silent, unnatural pause until it became second nature. It was during just such a habituated pause to look and listen that they noticed something critical—a tiny bit of a glove sticking up through the debris. Had they kept yelling, rather than pausing to listen and scan, they never would have found their teammate Rob, who was buried in the rubble. "I guess his hand was caught semi-vertically as he got smashed to the floor," Stephen said. The team was able to dig him out and drag him to safety seconds before the building collapsed.

Stephen and his fire brigade were lauded as heroes, and they absolutely are. Yet he attributes the rescue not to heroic determination but rather to the drills he and his team did to hone their default reactions and ensure they would respond wisely in an emergency.

It's safe to say that well-crafted habits have saved countless lives in fire emergencies, war zones, hospitals, and other high-stakes environments. But good habits are important for more than heroic rescues. When we need our autopilot to generate good results and can't rely on a default, the next-best option is to engineer a helpful habit. Drilling good behavior until it's second nature can help with everything from running a successful business to getting and staying healthy.

When behavioral scientists talk about habits, we often liken them to shortcuts. If you're a coffee drinker, think back to the first time you used a new coffee maker. It presumably required your full attention and took a bit of time as you figured out exactly where to pour the water and how many scoops of grinds you needed. But once you had done it morning after morning, it became habitual, and you could brew your morning joe quickly and without thinking.

Monotonous as it may sound, research in humans and other animals has proved that habits come from repeated drilling. Habit building is often less intentional than firefighters training to suit up or to pause and scan for signs of life, but it always involves many repetitions of an action, until it becomes not just familiar but instinctive. More often than not, the repetition that builds habits (such as nail-biting, smartphone checking, or coffee making) is accidental or mindless. If you want to develop good habits, or to replace bad habits with better ones, you'll be well-served to deliberately and repeatedly drill them, like a firefighter training to do the right thing in a high-pressure environment.

In now classic experiments run in the mid-twentieth century, the psychologist B. F. Skinner showed that if rats or pigeons were provided with repeated opportunities to engage in a behavior (like tapping a lever) followed by a consistent reward (like tasty treats), a habitual response would develop. The animals would learn to engage in the behavior and continue to do so even after they stopped getting rewards. It turns out that habits develop in people much as they do in rats and pigeons. But unlike rats and pigeons, we can intentionally train ourselves to have good habits, and we can help others train, too. The recipe is simple: the more we repeat an action in response to consistent cues and receive some reward (be it praise, relief, pleasure, or even cold hard cash), the more automatic our reactions become.

In fact, studies run by economists half a century after B. F. Skinner's famous experiments demonstrated that the same approach that worked with rats and pigeons could be used to help college students exercise more. To prove this, they recruited more than a hundred university students for a study about gym attendance and randomly assigned them to different groups. Some students were told they would earn 175 dollars if they attended an information session and two subsequent meetings, allowed the researchers to track their gym attendance, and visited the gym at least once in the next month. Others were told they would be paid the same 175 dollars only if they attended the information session and subsequent meetings, allowed their gym attendance to be tracked, and hit the gym at least *eight* times in the month ahead.

Unsurprisingly, the students who had to make eight gym visits to get paid exercised more than the others during that month. But what's really interesting is what happened after the payments stopped. The students who had just finished a month of unusually high exercise activity (those who had been offered 175 dollars for working out eight times) kept going to the gym much more often than the students who were paid to make only a single gym visit, even though no one was being paid to work out anymore. In fact, the eight-visit group members worked out roughly twice as often as the students in the other group over a seven-week follow-up period.

This finding supports a simple and largely accurate model of habit formation that has been popularized in bestsellers such as Charles Duhigg's *The Power of Habit* and James Clear's *Atomic Habits* (note that I say *largely* accurate—later in this chapter I'll explain a surprise twist that even I was startled to uncover). When a given behavior is repeated (or drilled) over and over in a consistent environment, and when positive feedback of any kind accompanies its execution, it tends to become instinctual. To revisit the example of making coffee in the morning, the consistent environment is your kitchen at breakfast time; the reward is fresh coffee; and the habit is the set of motions necessary to brew yourself a cup of joe. Or, to use an example made famous by Duhigg, the toothpaste industry cleverly habituated tooth brushing by associating this activity with a rewarding, minty fresh-ness that people came to crave each morning when standing in front of their bathroom sinks.

The beauty of good habits is that, like defaults that you can "set and forget," they take advantage of our inherent laziness.* Once honed, habits put good behaviors on autopilot so we engage in them without even thinking about it. In fact, in a fascinating series of six studies conducted with children and adults, psychologists Brian Galla and Angela Duckworth proved that positive habits are key to what we often mislabel "self-control." Those around us who seem to

---

*Our bad habits are similarly formed—unintentionally—through years of repetition and reward. For instance, anxious tics such as nail-biting or tooth grinding typically begin as a way to self-soothe through stress; they develop into sticky bad habits after enough repetition. Lunch from the vending machine begins as a quick fix in a pinch but is repeated with success often enough that it develops into an unthinking routine.

have tremendous willpower—people who run three miles every morning, are focused at work, hit the books hardest at school, and generally seem to make the right choices—are not actually endowed with a preternatural ability to resist temptation. Instead, good habits keep them from facing temptation head-on in the first place. They don't even *think* about making the wrong decision. They hit the gym each day because it's a habit, not because they carefully evaluated the pros and cons. They grab a smoothie for breakfast because it's their routine, not because they contemplated a greasy sausage biscuit but chose to exercise willpower. And they floss each night before bed because autopilot tells them to, not because they actively decide to invest time flossing today to avoid gum disease tomorrow.

In an ideal world, you would also put good decisions on autopilot. Once a good habit is successfully ingrained in your life, wise decisions become mindless. Then your tendency to take the path of least resistance helps you achieve your goals instead of standing in your way. You may not have thought about drilling behaviors like flossing and healthy eating the way you'd drill your skills as a pianist or firefighter, but it turns out that's just what you should do.

Unfortunately, adopting new habits isn't quite as simple as it sounds. Rewarding yourself for desirable behaviors and hitting repeat until your willpower is no longer needed to actively make the right decision is a strategy that sometimes works well. But I learned the hard way that this system operates seamlessly only in a world that's very predictable, which, unfortunately, is not the world most of us live in.

ELASTIC HABITS

Not long after a visit to Google's corporate headquarters inspired my work on fresh starts, I called my friends at the tech behemoth with a proposal. I knew that Google was eager to help its employees form better habits around wellness and, in particular, to encourage more employees to use its on-site gyms. So I pitched a low-cost strategy that I and my longtime collaborator, Harvard Business School professor John Beshears, were convinced could help.

John and I met as graduate students in a class that introduced me to the burgeoning field of behavioral economics and nudging. We quickly became friends and, later, coauthors. John is now a world-renowned economist responsible for much of the research on the many benefits of using defaults to help employees save for retirement. But, like me, he had grown eager to understand how people's tendency to take the path of least resistance could be harnessed to help improve important daily decisions that you can't just "set and forget" with a smart default—choices about technology use, diet, exercise, sleep, daily spending, and more.

It was clear to both of us that the answer had to do with habits. And since I knew Google was looking to help its employees form better habits around wellness—research shows that healthier employees are happier and more productive—John and I suspected the company might be a perfect test bed for an idea we'd developed about how to kick-start long-lasting habits more effectively.

Our idea had to do with the consistency of people's routines.

Imagine two people—let's call them Rachel and Fernando—who both want to exercise more regularly. Now say they both sign up for

a month of thrice-weekly sessions with personal trainers because
they hope to establish lasting workout habits. Since Rachel and Fernando have taken the same step toward their goal, it may seem that
they have the same chance of success.

But let's say that Rachel's trainer has a different philosophy from
Fernando's trainer. Rachel's trainer believes having a strict routine is
the best way to turn exercise into a habit. She asks Rachel to pick her
favorite workout time and tells her that they'll meet three days every
week at that time. By the end of the month, the trainer tells "Routine
Rachel," she'll have built a lasting habit.

Fernando, like Rachel, figures out his ideal daily workout time
and makes exercise plans with his personal trainer. But his trainer
believes flexibility is important and isn't too concerned about exactly
when Fernando exercises, so long as it happens three times each
week. She tells "Flexible Fernando" that varying the timing of his
visits to the gym will help him learn to roll with the punches and get
good at scheduling his workouts around conflicts. Fernando's trainer
assures him that by the end of a month, exercising three times a week
whenever he can fit the exercise in, he'll have built a lasting habit.

When John and I asked dozens of psychology professors at leading U.S. universities which hypothetical trainer they thought had the
better philosophy, there was a clear consensus. The vast majority predicted that visiting the gym at the same time on a strict routine would
produce more lasting exercise habits. John and I thought so, too.

So we were startled to discover that we had things all wrong.

John and I by no means developed our misguided intuition out of
the blue. A large body of evidence suggests that consistent routines
are important to producing lasting habits, including the studies I
mentioned earlier on B. F. Skinner's conditioning experiments with

rats and pigeons. Research also demonstrates that people are far more likely to take their medication consistently when they have regular pill-taking routines, and the vast majority of regular gym goers report exercising at a consistent time of day.

There is also a really entertaining study about popcorn consumption, of all things, that reinforces the importance of routines to habitual behavior. The habits expert Wendy Wood recruited theatergoers at a local cinema to watch and rate a series of short movies. These people were led to believe Wendy was studying their tastes in film, so when they were given free boxes of popcorn at the theater, they thought that it was simply a gesture of thanks for sharing their time and opinions.

In reality, though, the study was about the popcorn. Some of the boxes handed out contained fresh buttery popcorn. But some of the study participants received week-old popcorn that had been stored in plastic bags until it had lost all its crispness and buttery goodness. Unsurprisingly, people had no trouble differentiating between the good and bad popcorn. The bad stuff was universally described as disgusting. And the people who didn't usually eat popcorn at the movies behaved quite reasonably: they left the stale popcorn alone. But if they were lucky enough to get fresh snacks, they happily gobbled them up.

What's more surprising is Wendy's discovery that participants who *always* ate popcorn at the movies ate the same amount regardless of whether their serving was stale or a fresh, buttery treat. Their behavior relied on instinct and habit, not rational judgment. Fresh or stale, they ate the same amount because they were on autopilot. The movie theater was their cue that it was time to eat popcorn, so they ate it mindlessly.

To definitively establish this link between the cues that trigger habits and mindless behavior, Wendy's team reran the experiment in a different environment, showing music videos in a research lab (rather than movies in a theater), and the results were different. This time, people who always ate popcorn at the movies behaved just like moviegoers without a popcorn habit. Because they weren't encountering popcorn in the usual, routine way, autopilot didn't take over and lead them to eat the rubbery kernels that had been festering in plastic bags for a week.

Wendy told me that she actually wasn't at all surprised by these results. She knew from a career studying habits that repeating behaviors consistently in the same context (say, a movie theater) and getting a reward (say, tasty popcorn) will eventually cause us to respond to similar cues in well-rehearsed ways, even if the reward is no longer there (which is why some people will eat disgusting popcorn in a movie theater). "The cues could be other people; they could be the physical environment you're in; they could even be the time of day or some action you just did," Wendy says. "All those cues get tied with your response in your mind."

And fascinating research on rats has offered convergent evidence for this model of habit. It turns out that rats who have developed a heroin dependency react very differently if they receive an overdose of the drug in their familiar injection environment versus outside of it. If they're injected with an overdose in an unfamiliar environment, they're two times more likely to die. Why? When the rats are surrounded by their usual cues, their bodies react more habitually to the drug (the drug tolerance they've built up protects them), but in a foreign setting, their bodies underreact, which can be deadly. This research, though a bit macabre, vividly shows how a familiar environment affects the way mammals respond to familiar stimuli. We respond more habitually to drugs or eating popcorn or taking medication or exercising when we're in familiar circumstances. Familiarity breeds habit.*

All of this goes to say that John and I had good reason to suspect that if we wanted to help people build good habits around social media use, sleep, exercise, medication adherence, homework completion, firefighting, or parenting, getting them to develop consistent, stable, and familiar routines could be valuable. Going back to Rachel and Fernando, we had every reason to believe that Routine Rachel's trainer, who urged her to visit the gym at the same time each day, would help build a more lasting exercise habit than Flexible Fernando's trainer, who prioritized flexibility.

Our friends at Google loved the idea of helping their employees build lasting gym habits and graciously gave us the green light to test our theory at their on-site gyms.†

The study we ran involved more than twenty-five hundred Googlers at offices all around the United States. We measured participants' attendance at on-site gyms during a monthlong period when we were fiddling with their incentives, and for roughly forty weeks thereafter (to see what lasting effects, if any, our monthlong intervention had produced). The key feature of our study was a test we developed to see whether rewarding regularity in gym habits was the key to *lasting* change.

---

*This relates back to the idea of fresh starts—moments that break from the familiar and can disrupt habits.

†We were lucky to collaborate on this work with not only (former) Googler Jessica Wisdom but also two terrific Wharton doctoral students—Rob Mislavsky (now a professor at Johns Hopkins) and Sunny Lee.

Here's how that worked. Some employees were paid for exercising at the same time each day, while others were paid a bit less for exercising at any time.* Our study's design allowed us to compare people we had randomly assigned to behave like Routine Rachels (people who consistently worked out at the same time of day) with people we'd encouraged to act like Flexible Fernandos (exercising the same number of times per week as the Rachels, but on a less consistent schedule).

When the data came back, we were fairly certain that we would see evidence supporting the power of a strict, regular routine. So we were startled to learn that we had things all wrong.

Before explaining our error in logic, let me start by giving us a little credit—it's not that we had *everything* backward. Employees whom we rewarded for exercising at the same time each day did, in fact, form a slightly "stickier" habit around exercising specifically at their usual, planned time. When our monthlong program to kick-start exercise habits ended, employees who had been rewarded for regular exercise kept going to the gym at their regular time a bit more often than employees who had been rewarded for exercising whenever they felt like it.

But the big surprise was that Googlers we'd encouraged to hit the gym at a consistent time (the Routine Rachels) essentially built a habit around exercising only at that precise time. We had accidentally turned

---

*We not only randomized whether people earned money for any old gym visit or only visits at scheduled times, we also randomized how much we paid people for their gym visits. Some people made 3 dollars for their gym visits, while others made 7 dollars. As we expected, the more we paid, the more people exercised. Because our study's design produced variability both in when people exercised and how much they exercised, we could compare two employees who had been compelled to exercise at the same frequency during our monthlong intervention (say, twice each week), but with varying degrees of regularity in their routine.

them into inflexible automatons—transforming Routine Rachels into "Rigid Rachels." If they couldn't make it to the gym at their regular time, these Rigid Rachels were unlikely to go at all, either during or after our experiment. But both during and after our study, the employees we'd rewarded for exercising on a more flexible schedule kept working out a lot more at *other* times, too, not just at the time they'd said was most convenient. They had very clearly learned how to get to the gym even when their original plans fell through, and overall, that produced a "stickier" exercise habit.

While these results initially shocked me as well as many academic and corporate audiences I presented them to (I took pleasure in polling people at my seminars on their predictions and then revealing that almost everyone was wrong), I think this is one of the most important discoveries I've made in my research career.

Yes, forming stable routines is key to habit formation. But if we want to form the "stickiest" possible habits, we also need to learn how to roll with the punches, so we can be flexible when life throws us a curve ball. Too much rigidity is the enemy of a good habit.

Imagine that you're trying to develop a daily meditation routine. Ideally, you'd specify a time and place to meditate, such as in your office after lunch. As discussed in the last chapter, making a plan will help you remember to follow through. And research on habits shows that repeatedly meditating at the same time and in the same place, and rewarding yourself for it, will make it more automatic. But sometimes meditating in your office after lunch just won't work. Maybe you'll have a lunch meeting with a client off-site or a doctor's appointment during your lunch break. My research with John shows that if you can find a way to be flexible and meditate anyhow, under whatever circumstances you find yourself in, and reward yourself for getting it done, your meditation habit will become even stronger. By cultivating flexibility in your routine, your autopilot will become more robust: Your routine will be to meditate even under unideal circumstances. On the whole, you'll build a stickier, more lasting habit.

The more I thought about the results of my research with John, the more I recognized that at some subconscious level, I'd long appreciated the importance of flexibility to honing good habits. As a competitive teenage tennis player I applied this implicit insight in my daily practice sessions. When I worked out on the court, drilling forehands and backhands until the motions became second nature, I didn't always rehearse them in the same way. Sure, I practiced hitting hundreds of shots under ideal circumstances (when the ball came right to me and I had time to set up), but I also took great pains to hone my strokes under a wide range of conditions—pinned behind the baseline, running back from the net to chase after a lob, racing forward to hit a drop shot. By drilling my shots under such varied circumstances, it became second nature to hit the ball comfortably no matter where I found myself during a match. The same lesson turns out to be true of any habit. If you practice it only in the ideal environment, it won't be as useful or robust as a habit honed more flexibly.

I remain convinced that by deliberately building good habits, we can harness our inherent laziness to make positive changes to our behavior. But it's now clear to me that to put good behavior on autopilot, we can't cultivate it in only one, specific way. The most versatile and robust habits are formed when we train ourselves to make the best decision, no matter the circumstances.

DAY IN AND DAY OUT

We all know Ben Franklin as a Founding Father, philosopher, scientist, writer, printer, and, perhaps most famously, as the man whose kite first harnessed electricity. I'm particularly enamored of him since he founded the University of Pennsylvania, where I work, and was a pretty savvy behavioral scientist on the side. (Who can disagree with "Haste makes waste" or "Well done is better than well said"?)

In his late teens, however, Franklin spent a couple of years as a philandering wastrel in London. He spent frivolously, overindulged at the local taverns, and generally engaged in debauchery. It wasn't until his voyage home to Philadelphia, during which his ship hit some unlucky currents that lengthened the trip from a few weeks to more than two months, that he reportedly made a plan to turn himself around.

All that extra time for reflection apparently helped young Ben Franklin decide to make a fresh start. Famously, he developed a careful strategy for cultivating a set of virtues that he thought would lead to a productive and fulfilling life. With the goal of turning righteous behavior into a habit, Franklin created a system of charts to track his daily success or failure in exhibiting thirteen different virtues: temperance, silence, order, resolution, frugality, industry, sincerity, justice, moderation, cleanliness, tranquility, chastity, and humility. He would penalize failures with a black mark and reward successes with a nice blank slate. As history shows, Franklin did manage to make something of himself, after all (to put it mildly). Perhaps his charts are partially responsible.

Roughly three hundred years later, the comedian Jerry Seinfeld swears by a similar philosophy. Because most jokes are mediocre, and it takes many tries to produce a good one, Seinfeld has committed himself to generating a new joke every day, and he charts his progress much as Franklin did. Seinfeld's motto is "Don't break the streak."

Ben Franklin and Jerry Seinfeld are interesting case studies for many reasons. First, both recognized the power of habit and saw that to create new habits, they would have to repeat their actions again and again.

Second, both men religiously *tracked* their efforts. Research suggests that by tracking your exercise, your joke production, or even your virtuousness, you'll increase your chances of changing your behavior. That's in part because tracking a behavior helps you avoid forgetting to do it until it becomes second nature. It's also a nice way to ensure you celebrate your successes and hold yourself accountable for failure. When your successes and failures are right there in your face, it's difficult not to feel proud when you've done what you set out to do, and a little ashamed when you haven't.

Both Ben Franklin and Jerry Seinfeld also worried a lot about lapses in their routines. Recent research suggests that anything more than a short lapse in a behavior we hope to make habitual (say, multiple missed visits to the gym rather than just one) can be costly. Seinfeld's mantra "Don't break the streak" is astute. It also helps explain the logic behind twenty-eight-pill packages of birth control. Scientifically speaking, the pills are necessary only on the first twenty-one days of a twenty-eight-day menstrual cycle. However, most birth control packages include seven sugar pills along with twenty-one hormone pills to ensure that people on birth control won't fall out of the habit of taking the medication during their "off" week. While a better form of contraception would involve a one-time-only dose (such as a vaccine for shingles but reversible), the next-best option is a daily dose.*

The main lesson I hope you'll remember from this chapter is just that. The ideal solution to any problem stemming from our inherent laziness is a single-dose solution—a default. If you can "set it and forget it," whatever change you're trying to create will be quite easy to make.†

Unfortunately, we often can't rely on onetime solutions. When laziness is working against us and a default can't produce lasting change—when there's no onetime vaccine to cure what ails us—the next-best option is to engineer a habit. Engineering habits means relying on repetition or "drilling" to develop a consistent response to familiar cues, while rewarding ourselves for each success.

There's some intriguing new research suggesting we can piggy-

---

*IUDs are the closest thing we have to a birth control vaccine and they have grown vastly in popularity, particularly as evidence of their safety has accumulated (Erin Magner, "Why the IUD Is Suddenly Queen of the Contraceptive World," Well + Good, February 7, 2019, accessed August 20, 2020, www.wellandgood.com/iud-birth-control -comeback).

†Penn Medicine figured this out quickly after the success of their generic prescription default, and they found other big wins by deploying a similar logic. The Nudge Unit that Mitesh started has since cut prescriptions of habit-forming opioids in half by defaulting the number of pills given in each script to ten (instead of the usual thirty-day dose) (M. K. Delgado et al., "Association between Electronic Medical Record Implementation of Default Opioid Prescription Quantities and Prescribing Behavior in Two Emergency Departments," *Journal of General Internal Medicine* 33, no. 4 [2018]: 409–11, DOI:10.1007/s11606-017-4286-5). They also more than quintupled the referral rate of cardiac patients to rehab by making this clinical best practice the default (Srinath Adusumalli et al., "Abstract 19699: A Change in Cardiac Rehabilitation Referral Defaults From Opt-In to Opt-Out Increases Referral Rates among Patients with Ischemic Heart Disease," *Circulation* 136, no. suppl_1 [2017], DOI:10.1161/circ.136.suppl_1.19699).

back new habits on old ones by linking whatever we hope to start doing regularly—such as push-ups or eating fruit—with something we already do habitually, such as drinking a morning cup of coffee or leaving for work. In a small but promising recent study, people attempting to kick-start a flossing habit were more successful when they were prompted to floss *after* brushing their teeth, rather than before. If you think about the power of cues, you'll recognize that putting a toothbrush back into its holder became the cue that triggered people to pick up their floss. The new habit piggybacked on the old one.

I've used this strategy myself. When my life as a new mom was too hectic to accommodate trips to the gym, I knew I needed to develop a new daily exercise habit. So I piggybacked seven-minute workouts onto my already well-established morning washroom routine, and I rarely missed a day.

Linking a new behavior that you'd like to turn into a habit with other habits that already exist in your life makes it easier to follow through during the critical early phase of habit development. It also helps if we track our performance and reward ourselves for success, strive to maintain streaks, and build flexibility into our routines so that whatever roadblocks we encounter don't impede our progress.

With these insights in mind, it's possible to turn laziness on its head. The path of least resistance, that consummate liability when you're looking to change, can instead become an asset.

—————— **Chapter Takeaways** ——————

- Laziness, or the tendency to follow the path of least resistance, can stand in the way of change.

- A default is the outcome you'll get if you don't actively choose another option (such as the standard factory settings that come with a new computer). If you select defaults wisely (say, setting your browser's homepage to your work email instead of Facebook), you can turn laziness into an asset that facilitates change (say, wasting less time on social media).

- Habits are like default settings for our behavior. They put good behavior on autopilot. The more you repeat an action in familiar circumstances and receive some reward (be it praise, relief, pleasure, or cold hard cash), the more habitual and automatic your reactions become in those situations.

- Too much rigidity is the enemy of a good habit. By allowing for flexibility in your routines, your autopilot can become flexible, too. You will find you respond consistently even under unideal circumstances. Overall, you'll build "stickier," more lasting habits.

- Tracking your behavior can facilitate habit building. It helps you avoid forgetting to follow through and ensures that you celebrate your successes and hold yourself accountable for failures.

- Aim for streaks. Anything more than a short lapse in a behavior you hope to make habitual (say, multiple missed

visits to the gym, as opposed to just one) can keep a new
habit from forming or disrupt an existing one.

• Piggybacking new habits on old ones can help with habit
  formation. Link whatever you hope to start doing regularly (such as push-ups or eating fruit) with something you
  already do habitually (such as drinking a morning cup of
  coffee or leaving for work).

CHAPTER 6

Confidence

When I walked into my adviser Max Bazerman's office midway through my doctoral studies in 2007, my slumped shoulders and dejected expression telegraphed just how devastated I was feeling. A manuscript I'd spent the last two years crafting under his guidance had been returned from the journal I'd submitted it to with the word every scholar dreads most stamped on top—"Rejected." Notes from three experts in my field accompanied the verdict, highlighting the many flaws in my research. "I'll never get it published," I lamented.

As I awaited Max's advice, I scanned his office. There's nothing unusual about the old journals that line his shelves, but very few scholars can display anything like the floor-to-ceiling canvas poster of academic progeny that hangs on Max's wall—a "family tree" that a former student gave him for his fiftieth birthday. Max's name is emblazoned on the top, with each branch beneath him representing one of the dozens of world-class scholars he's mentored, followed by their mentees and then their mentees. The people on that academic family tree are now senior professors at Harvard, Columbia, NYU, Stanford, Duke, Cornell, UCLA, Berkeley, and Northwestern, among other prestigious schools. (Notably, in a field dominated by men, the majority of his former students are women.*) Though I had hoped to someday join the ranks of the successful former students on Max's chart, the weight of this fresh failure made me doubt I ever would.

I braced myself for the worst. It seemed likely Max would suggest I rip up my manuscript and start over. But he offered a calm and reassuring smile and leaned back in his chair.

In his usual easy and matter-of-fact tone, Max maintained that my work was strong and would unquestionably be published. I simply needed to try again. "Spend the next forty-eight hours doing everything you can to address the critiques, and then send it off to another journal," he urged. "The worst thing you can do is sit on bad news."

Somewhat stunned but utterly relieved, I agreed to get right back to work. "Excellent!" said Max, radiating enthusiasm.

By the time I arrived at Wharton two years later as an assistant professor (having successfully published my paper), that uplifting exchange was a distant memory. But successfully advising students was very much top of mind; I was eager to begin helping my own set of graduate students achieve their potential. A roadblock quickly became apparent, however: Early in my first year I discovered that many PhD students in my orbit were unhappy and ultimately unsuccessful. Even when they arrived with stellar recommendations, impressive academic credentials, and sky-high hopes, talented doctoral students

---

*Max's inclusive mentoring style is so legendary in academia that he was featured prominently in the book *The Person You Mean to Be: How Good People Fight Bias* (HarperCollins, 2018).

often grew demoralized when they began facing critiques of their research, and many never recovered their footing. A few years later, I learned this pattern was widespread in academia. A survey that had just been released showed that the average mental health metrics of students in leading social science PhD programs looked similar to those of people incarcerated in U.S. prisons!

I reached out to Max to ask what tricks he had up his sleeve. If I could adopt his mentoring techniques, I was sure I could help more Wharton students become academic stars. "The computer scientist in me assumes there must be some algorithms or 'rules of thumb' you've found helpful over the years (and some things you've discovered really don't work)," I wrote in a 2012 email.

Max's response was typically humble but also a touch disappointing. After thanking me for the praise, he insisted it was unwarranted. Though he offered a few tips on how to help PhD students achieve more, the main thrust of his message was that great students simply found him. "I've worked with students who range from very smart to spectacular," he said. In Max's view, it was the talent of his students, not the quality of his advising, that made him look so good.

I couldn't believe that my former mentor had no strategies I could emulate to help my PhD students excel, so I gathered his tips and supplemented them with my own observations to create a list of best practices. Max responded to emails within hours, not days, and he read draft manuscripts quickly, too, offering valuable comments on how to revise and improve them. Check. I could do that. He held weekly group meetings where his students shared feedback with one another on their research. He hosted dinners for visiting faculty where students could get to know leaders in the field. He taught a doctoral seminar, sharing important research and explaining in detail why it mattered. Check. Check. Check. Maybe helping more PhD students stay motivated and achieve their goals wouldn't be so hard.

But as I spent more time around other doctoral advisers, I realized that many academic mentors checked the same boxes. The formula I'd written down simply didn't explain why Max's students were so extraordinarily successful, winning him every major mentoring award in our field.

I also grew doubtful that great students simply found their way to Max. I learned that he had turned away only two students in his thirty-year career, and it seemed unlikely that nearly every aspiring academic who walked through his door had the talent, confidence, and grit to succeed where so many failed without excellent coaching. There had to be something more to Max's recipe.

WANT SOME ADVICE?

Imagine you're at a family gathering. You're catching up with your aunt and a few cousins when you look over to see your three-year-old grab a toy away from another child and then smack her playmate on the arm. After you send your toddler off for a time-out, your cousin Betty pulls you aside and says, "You know, I think you could have handled that better." She goes on to give you a lesson in disciplining children. How would you feel? Odds are, you wouldn't be particularly grateful for the pro tip. You'd probably be demoralized or annoyed or both. No one likes to be lectured.

What's ironic is that even though we can all see that receiving this kind of unsolicited advice is a giant downer, most of us have followed

Cousin Betty's script at one point or another. It's common to give out advice when we see someone struggling to achieve a goal. We often think guidance is just the thing they're looking for, whether they ask for it or not.

A few years ago, I met a graduate student who had a hunch we'd gotten the formula backward. Lauren Eskreis-Winkler, a former competitive pianist and Ivy Leaguer, was always a high achiever and found it baffling that so many of her talented peers struggled to meet their goals. As a PhD student in psychology, she wanted to understand what separates top performers from the rest of us, so she began collecting data. She surveyed Americans struggling to save more money, to lose weight, to control their tempers, and to find employment. She also interviewed salespeople at Aflac (the insurer best known for its quirky commercials featuring a talking duck) as well as high school students in Philadelphia, New Jersey, and even Macedonia. She asked everyone what might motivate them to be more successful at work, at home, and in their academic pursuits.

And as she sifted through her data, Lauren made a surprising discovery: when it came to being more successful, people had plenty of good ideas for how to do it. Even underperforming salespeople, C students, unemployed job seekers, and spendthrifts struggling to save consistently offered smart strategies for improving their circumstances. Students made suggestions ranging from the mundane ("Turn off your phone when you're studying") to the creative ("Put candy at the bottom of a worksheet, and when you finish, you can eat it"). People with money problems advised "Don't pay with a credit card." Job seekers suggested keeping résumés up-to-date and carrying them at all times. Almost everyone knew what to do to overcome their problems; they just weren't doing it.

Lauren began to suspect that this failure to act wasn't related to a lack of knowledge, but rather to self-doubt—what the legendary Stanford psychologist Al Bandura has called "a lack of self-efficacy." Self-efficacy is a person's confidence in their ability to control their own behavior, motivation, and social circumstances. I talked in earlier chapters about our alarming capacity for overconfidence, and how it can interfere with attaining our goals. But this is the reverse problem: goal strivers are sometimes plagued by insecurity. In fact, a lack of self-efficacy can prevent us from setting goals in the first place.

You can probably think of examples from your own life—moments when you (or someone you know) didn't achieve your full potential because the task at hand seemed too daunting. Maybe you're a long-distance runner who's never attempted a marathon because you don't think you're quite athletic enough to cover 26.2 miles. Maybe you have a coworker who doesn't speak up in meetings because she doesn't think people will value what she has to say.

Research confirms the obvious: when we don't believe we have the capacity to change, we don't make as much progress changing. One study demonstrated that when trying to lose weight, people who report more confidence in their ability to change their eating and exercise habits are more successful. Another study similarly showed that science and engineering undergraduates with higher self-efficacy earn higher grades and are less likely to drop out of their majors.

Of course, some aspirations really are out of reach for most people, such as becoming the next Toni Morrison, Marie Curie, or Bill Gates. But many of us stumble in pursuit of far more realistic goals, such as learning a foreign language or getting in shape. Understanding what gives us the confidence to push forward in the face of discouragement, and how we can instill that confidence in other people, can be important for anyone hoping to change and help others do the same.

Recognizing this gave Lauren a creative idea. Too often, we assume that the obstacle to change in others is *ignorance*, and so we offer advice to mend that gap. But what if the problem isn't ignorance but *confidence*—and our unsolicited wisdom isn't making things better but worse?

As a psychologist, Lauren knew that people are quick to infer implicit messages in the actions of others, even when no such message is intended. She realized that in giving advice, we might be inadvertently conveying to people that we don't think they can succeed on their own—implying that we view them as so hopeless that two minutes of advice will be worth more than all they've learned from attempting to solve their own problems. So she wondered: What if we flipped the script?

If giving advice can destroy confidence, then asking people who are struggling to be advisers instead of advisees might be a better approach. Encouraging someone to share their wisdom conveys that they're intelligent, capable of helping others, a good role model, and the kind of person who succeeds. It shows that we believe in them. In theory, being asked to write just a few words of guidance to someone else might give people the confidence to achieve their *own* objectives.

Lauren ran survey after survey of Americans with unmet goals. Some were striving to save more, others to control their tempers, get fit, or find new jobs. Time and again, she found two things. First, when asked directly, most people predicted that receiving advice would be more motivating than giving it, which explains why we're all the targets of so much unsolicited advice. But when she examined the accuracy of this belief, using controlled experiments, she found that it was wrong. Just as she'd come to suspect, prompting goal seekers to *offer* advice led them to feel more motivated than when they were *given* the very same caliber of advice.

Of course, motivation is a far cry from behavior change. It was possible that Lauren's idea wouldn't really help people reach their goals. But it seemed promising enough to warrant a larger test. So, in the winter of 2018, I teamed up with Lauren, Angela Duckworth, and Dena Gromet on a massive experiment aimed at helping students achieve their academic goals.

On the day of the experiment, shortly after the start of a new school term, nearly two thousand students across seven Florida high schools walked into a computer lab with their teachers. Some simply filled out a few short digital questionnaires. But others were invited to do something quite out of the ordinary. All their lives, these students, like all students, had been given advice in school—"stay focused in class," "do more practice problems before tests," and "always turn your homework in on time." Today would be different. This time, they were being asked for *their* advice.

This lucky group of students was invited to offer guidance to their younger peers through a ten-minute online survey. They were peppered with questions such as "What helps you avoid procrastinating?" "Where do you go to do focused studying?" and "What general tips would you give someone hoping to do better in school?"

After completing these surveys, students were left to their own devices for the remainder of the academic term. Then, at the end of the marking period, we downloaded their grades in the class they'd told us was most important to them as well as their grades in math (according to Angela, kids say they prefer eating broccoli to doing their math homework!). Lo and behold, our strategy had worked. The students who had given just a few minutes of advice performed better in these classes than other students.

To be clear, giving a handful of study tips to other kids didn't turn C students into valedictorians, but it did boost performance for high schoolers from every walk of life. Strong students, weak students, students in the free lunch program, and students from wealthier families all saw small improvements in their grades after advising peers.

And anecdotally, we also heard that giving advice seemed to bring students joy. High schoolers in our study told their teachers they'd never been asked for their insights before and loved having the chance to share. "Could we do this again soon?" they prodded hopefully.

The more Lauren reflected on her research on the power of advice giving, the more it made sense. She recognized that being asked to give advice conveyed to people that more was expected of them, boosting their confidence. And based on the interviews she'd conducted, Lauren also knew that even on the spot, with no time to think hard about it—people were capable of producing useful insights about how to better tackle the same goals they, themselves, struggled with. Recall how much good advice she garnered even from underperforming salesmen, mediocre students, and other strivers.

This is a key reason why giving advice to others tends to help *us*. Another is that we tend to tailor the advice we give based on personal experience. If asked for dieting suggestions, a vegan will offer plant-based tips. If asked about staying in shape, a busy executive will recommend an efficient exercise regimen. In short, when someone asks for guidance, we tell them to do what *we* would find useful. And after offering that advice to others, we feel hypocritical if we don't try it ourselves. In psychology, there's something called the "saying-is-believing effect." Thanks to cognitive dissonance, after you say something to someone else, you're more likely to believe it yourself.

This idea—that giving advice can be more important to your success than receiving it—was echoed by the legendary drummer Mike Mangini when he appeared on my podcast in 2019. He talked about how he developed the confidence he needed to rise to stardom. Now the lead drummer for world-famous heavy metal band Dream Theater, Mike took a path to the top that was anything but straight. He spent the 1980s as a software engineer, practicing incessantly on the drums at night and on the weekends, daydreaming of a big career in music with little hope of achieving his goal.

Then something changed. When other drummers in a shared practice space unexpectedly began knocking on Mike's door and asking him to give them lessons, their requests gave Mike a new-found confidence. If so many people thought he had a special talent, maybe he did. Mike quit his day job and devoted himself full time to drumming. Today, he's one of the best-known drummers in the business. He attributes his success, in no small part, to being asked to give *other people* advice.

Here's a question you might have, though: What if no one ever asks you for advice? How can you use Lauren's insight to help yourself succeed when it depends on something out of your control—namely, the solicitousness of others?

The good news is that it's possible to harness the power of advice giving to help yourself. One way is by forming an advice club: a group of people whose members regularly consult one another for help. I know this works because I did it myself, long before I even knew about Lauren's research.

Back in 2015, I learned from Carnegie Mellon economist Linda Babcock that women tend to bear the brunt of low-prestige office tasks, such as planning the holiday party, taking notes at meetings, and serving on endless committees. (This is true across industries and cultures.) In order to save herself from this fate, Linda formed an advice club with four female colleagues so that they could help one another say "no" more often. I was so impressed by the idea that I asked two faculty friends—Modupe Akinola and Dolly Chugh—to join a similar club with me: we pledged to help one another make tough calls whenever any of us got invited to do something time-consuming outside of our teaching and research responsibilities. Now, whenever one of us is asked to deliver a talk, write a blog post, or give an interview, we reach out to our "No Club" to discuss whether the opportunity is worthwhile and to get advice on how to politely but firmly turn it down if it isn't.

The solicited advice I receive from the club is invaluable. But I've also reaped huge benefits from the advice I've given. Helping my colleagues decide when it's right for them to say no has boosted my confidence that I can judge for *myself* when it's right to say no, so I lean on the club less and less with each passing year. I've also benefited from the "saying-is-believing effect." After encouraging someone else not to waste her precious time giving an invited lecture on a topic outside her core area of expertise, I would feel pretty ridiculous saying yes to a similar invitation myself.

You might consider forming your own advice clubs with friends who are struggling to achieve goals similar to your own. As you provide and receive (solicited) advice, you'll boost one another's confidence and unearth ideas that help with your own problems. Another simple suggestion is to turn advice giving inside out when you're facing a challenge. Ask yourself: "If a friend or colleague were struggling with the same problem, what advice would I offer?" Taking this perspective can help you approach the same problem with greater confidence and insight.

If you're a manager, it might seem counterintuitive to place underperforming employees into mentoring roles. But it could boost their lagging performance. It's no accident that well-regarded programs that are designed to help us achieve lasting change, such as Alcoholics Anonymous (AA), encourage members to mentor one another. People in AA get another AA member as a "sponsor" when they sign up, but the sponsor isn't just there to help a mentee stay sober. Lauren's research on advice giving suggests that becoming a sponsor can help you stay sober *yourself* by boosting your self-confidence. Not only that, thinking deeply about the best way to stay away from alcohol so that you can offer guidance and being accountable to someone else should also strengthen your own commitment to sobriety. Mentoring programs in companies and schools serve this dual purpose, too, whether or not they were designed with these additional benefits in mind.

Looking back on my experience as Max Bazerman's doctoral student, I now realize that he understood, at least intuitively if not consciously, the power of giving advice to others. Of course, when prompted, Max offers clear and direct advice to his students. But it's offered sparingly, and his advice is rarely unsolicited (unless he's telling you about an opportunity you might not be aware of). More often, he provides students with chances to share their own suggestions. And Max strongly encourages his more senior mentees to work on research with his newest advisees, which, as you can now see, helps the advanced doctoral students just as much as the newcomers.

I learned from Lauren that once you view mentoring as a two-way street, you're armed with a new way to promote positive change. But that wasn't all I learned. Lauren also helped me appreciate how critical it is to consider what we're conveying *implicitly* when we interact with people who are trying to change. That insight helped her understand why unsolicited advice is so often perceived as criticism. But in other research, that insight turns out to be even more illuminating.

GREAT EXPECTATIONS

One day in mid-2004, eighty-four hotel housekeepers in Boston and Colorado showed up for work and went about their jobs as usual. Each housekeeper cleaned more than a dozen rooms, stripping the linens from the beds, re-making them with fresh sheets, vacuuming the floors, scrubbing the bathroom sinks, tubs, tiles, and toilets, and replacing towels, soap, and shampoo. But that day there was a slight twist to their workflow. After they finished with their usual tasks, the housekeepers had their weight, height, and blood pressure measured and were each asked to fill out a series of questionnaires. They were participating in a study led by the psychologist Alia Crum and her mentor, Ellen Langer.

While the housekeepers who volunteered for the study knew that it had something to do with their health and well-being, they were unaware of the exact hypothesis the researchers were testing. Alia and Ellen weren't just trying to learn about the housekeepers' health. They also wanted to explore the way our expectations can shape our reality.

The researchers shared a crucial bit of information with half of the housekeepers. This group learned that their work helped them get the amount of daily exercise that's recommended by health experts. The other half weren't told anything at all.

When Alia and Ellen followed up four weeks later, they discovered something remarkable. Although none of the housekeepers in the study had changed their daily routines—they weren't exercising more outside of work or cleaning additional rooms—the workers who'd learned about the health benefits of their jobs had lost two pounds on average, their blood pressure had dropped, and they reported feeling like they'd exercised more than usual. Meanwhile, the housekeepers who were kept in the dark about the health benefits of their work had not seen their health change a bit.

How could it be that one group saw health improvements while the other didn't when no one in the study changed their old routines? The answer is straightforward, though subtle: something critical *had* changed. The housekeepers who learned about the health benefits of their job had shifted the way they *viewed* their work, and that altered the way they felt about it and approached it. Suddenly, they looked at lifting a mattress not just as a chore, but as exercise. Vacuuming was a workout, as was cleaning the windows. Knowing that their work could keep them healthy changed the way the housekeepers experienced their jobs and likely increased the vigor and enthusiasm with which they approached each opportunity to burn calories.

The study's key revelation was simple, but profound: Our expectations shape our outcomes.

This turns out to be a good summary of one of the most influential discoveries psychologists have made in the past fifty years—that how we *think* about something affects how it *is*. We now know that believing a useless sugar pill is medication alleviates many maladies, that attributing the butterflies in your stomach to excitement rather than anxiety will make you a better public speaker, and that believing that people expect you to do well on a test can improve your score.

If you're wondering how this can possibly work, scientists like Alia Crum have a lot of answers. They've shown that our expectations about what will happen can influence what actually happens in four key ways. First, our beliefs can change our emotions. If you have positive expectations, that often generates positive feelings, which have a host of physiological benefits such as alleviating stress and reducing blood pressure. And that can make a big difference in what happens next.

Our beliefs can also redirect our attention. Take the housekeepers described above. If they started paying closer attention to the ways in which their work was like exercise, they may have interpreted their physical exhaustion more positively throughout a long workday, helping them press on.

There is also evidence that beliefs can change motivation. Again, consider the housekeepers. Their motivation to get high-quality exercise on the job likely increased once they started thinking of work as an opportunity to improve their fitness.

And finally, beliefs can affect our physiology—not just through our emotions, but directly. For example, when Alia and a different team of collaborators offered the same milkshake to the same people at two separate gatherings, telling them on one occasion that they were drinking a high-fat, high-calorie "indulgent" milkshake and on the other occasion that they were drinking a low-fat, low-calorie "sensible" milkshake, they made a remarkable discovery. When their study participants thought they were gulping down more calories, they produced less of a gut peptide that stimulates hunger. Their beliefs changed their body's physical reaction to the very same drink.*

By changing our emotions, our attention, our motivation, and our physiology, our beliefs can powerfully shape our experiences.

One of my favorite stories illustrating the power of our beliefs involves the Berkeley math doctoral student George Dantzig. The story goes that George arrived late to his statistics class in 1939 and assumed the two math problems on the chalkboard were homework. So he copied them down to solve that night. He found the problems more difficult than usual, but he returned to class with the answers after a few days and apologized to his professor for taking so long. Soon afterward, the professor tracked George down, brimming with excitement. As it turned out, George had solved two "unsolvable" open problems in statistical theory because he believed they were merely difficult homework assignments with known answers.

Had George been aware that these problems were stumping the world's best mathematicians, he might not have come up with the proofs. The accident of being late set him up to do something extraordinary. And that, in turn, helped change his life, launching him on a path to a professorship at Stanford University and an academic career filled with other major discoveries.

Because George *believed* he was supposed to find a solution, he did. Because the housekeepers in Alia and Ellen's study *viewed* their work as exercise, they treated it that way, with positive consequences

---

*A subsequent study showed that describing stress as enhancing (rather than as debilitating) changed people's physiological responses to stressful events, increasing their secretion of hormones that moderate responses to stress and promote growth (Alia J. Crum et al., "The Role of Stress Mindset in Shaping Cognitive, Emotional, and Physiological Responses to Challenging and Threatening Stress," *Anxiety, Stress & Coping* 30, no. 4 [2017]: 379–95, DOI:10.1080/10615806.2016.1275585).

for their health. What we *think* we're capable of is crucial when it comes to behavior change.

And of course, our beliefs do not come out of the blue. The feedback and reinforcement we get from the people around us play a key role in shaping our beliefs about our own abilities.

I think this insight can help explain another critical ingredient in Max Bazerman's mentoring algorithm—something he mentioned as soon as I sought his counsel on how to be a good mentor, but that I'd failed to pick up on.

Max had insisted that there wasn't anything special about him that helped his students succeed. It was something special about his *students*. When I emailed asking for his mentoring secrets, he'd explained that his students ranged "from very smart to spectacular." His unshakable faith that each student he advised had remarkable talents, I now realized, was a bedrock of Max's advising success.

As Max's students begin to confront the challenges that are inevitable in any competitive career, they rarely grapple with the kind of doubt that plagues most who pursue a PhD because of Max's confidence in them. Next to the unwavering love of my parents, there was probably nothing I felt more secure about in my twenties than the fact that my adviser believed I was destined for success. Max made it clear to all of his students that he knew we'd succeed. And, lo and behold, we did.

I've since learned that many great leaders have a similar contagious belief that the people on their team will grow and flourish. Jack Welch, the legendary CEO who presided over decades of extraordinary profitability at GE, was well-known for his devotion to developing his employees' leadership skills and his belief in their capacity to improve. Many celebrated coaches operate the same way.

Pete Carroll, who led the Seattle Seahawks to victory in the 2014 Super Bowl, is widely admired for the confidence he has in his players to work hard and get better.

But we don't always have the good fortune of someone standing by our side convincing us that we have what it takes to reach our goals. Nor can we necessarily arrange for the arrival of a credible cheerleader on demand. What then? How can we overcome the self-doubt that inevitably accompanies bumps in the road?

RECOVERING FROM FAILURE

When pursuing a goal, it can be easy to get discouraged. Research on the aptly named "what-the-hell effect" has demonstrated that even small failures, such as missing a daily diet goal by a few calories, can lead to downward spirals in behavior—such as eating a whole apple pie. This will sound familiar if you've ever given in to temptation in the morning (say, grabbing a proffered donut at a breakfast meeting) and then, having slipped up once, decided "What the hell. I already goofed, so all bets are off." A minor mistake can tank your confidence, making you believe you'll never succeed. Unfortunately, the more ambitious your goals, the higher the risk of a small but ultimately devastating failure.

Marissa Sharif, one of my Wharton colleagues, has a clever approach she uses to dodge the what-the-hell effect and maintain her confidence even when her plans veer off track.

For more than a decade, Marissa has held herself to the ambitious goal of running every day, which helps her stay healthy and deal with the stress of a fast-paced career. But she's long been wary of the what-the-hell effect, recognizing that a missed jog could easily spiral into a series of skipped workouts and eventually she might stop running altogether. In an effort to dodge this kind of unraveling, she came up with a clever idea. Marissa allows herself two emergencies each week because she knows she won't *always* be able to lace up her sneakers in the morning.* She might have a late dinner, be on the road for a conference, or simply not have the energy for a run. If she can't squeeze in a workout, she lets herself take one of her two mulligans, and this flexibility keeps her on track (a bit like our Flexible Fernando).

While it might seem like she'd be tempted to take a mulligan even when things aren't dire, the opposite is true. Most weeks, Marissa never uses one. She told me that she always sticks to her workout schedule at the beginning of the week in case something more important comes up later, and when it doesn't, which is most of the time, she finds herself running all seven days.

It eventually occurred to Marissa that maybe, just maybe, her personal approach to nipping self-doubt in the bud whenever she faced a minor failure could be used to help all of us get a little better at achieving more. After all, if we allow ourselves the occasional do-over, we might avoid crises of confidence when we encounter inevitable setbacks.

To test the depth and range of her strategy, Marissa and a collaborator cooked up a study involving hundreds of people who were paid to visit a website and do thirty-five annoying tasks (solving CAPTCHAs—those tests used online to "prove that you're human")

---

*Although against the formal rules of the game, many (perhaps most) casual golfers occasionally allow one another to take a second shot, or "mulligan," with no stroke penalty when a first attempt goes awry. The idea of a penalty-free second try is so popular, in fact, that mulligans are a formal component of a number of popular modern games, ranging from Magic to Pokémon.

every day for a week in exchange for 1 dollar a batch. These workers were randomly assigned to three groups. Some got the tough goal of completing their work every day of the week. Others were given the easier objective of completing their work just five days out of seven. Finally, a third, "mulligan" group was told to complete the assignment every day, but those in this group were permitted to excuse up to two missed days as emergencies. Everyone knew they would get a 5-dollar bonus if they managed to achieve their goal.

The chance to declare an emergency proved invaluable. A whopping 53 percent of those in the mulligan group hit their goal, compared with just 26 percent in the (objectively identical) easy category and 21 percent of participants with the seven-days-per-week goal.

These findings highlight how important it is to make explicit allowances for emergencies. Perhaps it's no surprise that lots of programs aimed at healthier eating incorporate similar ideas into their design, allowing "goal cushions" and "cheat meals" so that self-confidence survives small mistakes.*

If this idea feels familiar to the concept of elastic habits introduced in the last chapter, it should. Allowing for emergencies is another way of preventing excess rigidity from torpedoing successful attempts at change. It gives your ego a means of bouncing back from the inevitable, occasional failure.

Another way to prepare for unavoidable disappointments on the

---

*WW (formerly Weight Watchers), for example, has set up a system of SmartPoints to rate foods based on nutritional value. People who use the WW program are allowed a certain number of SmartPoints per day based on their health goals. The people who designed the program understand that humans aren't perfect, so they deliberately added in a "cushion"—a few extra points for emergencies ("Starter Guide: Everything You Need to Know about SmartPoints," WW, accessed October 5, 2020, www.weightwatch ers.com/us/how-it-works/smartpoints).

path to change is by having a proper understanding of what failure means in the first place. It turns out that the way we interpret failure has a lot to do with future success. Stanford's Carol Dweck has become legendary for proving this. In dozens of studies with students and adults, she's demonstrated that having a "growth mind-set"—the belief that abilities, including intelligence, are not fixed and that effort influences a person's potential—predicts success. Those of us who think we're born with a fixed capacity for achievement can fall victim to defeatism, putting in little effort to learn from failures and grow. But those of us who view ourselves as works in progress, capable of improvement, exert vastly more effort in the face of setbacks. We seek out challenges, learn from failure, and generally achieve far more as a result.

Happily, the mind-set we're born with doesn't have to be the one we're stuck with. We can use clever tricks like Marissa's to keep us from being so hard on ourselves when we face setbacks, and we can also change the way we interpret failure.

Carol Dweck's protégé, the University of Texas psychologist David Yeager, has worked with collaborators to teach high school and college freshmen that failure is a learning experience—and that through hard work, we can enrich our intelligence in any arena. In one study, thousands of high school freshmen received this encouraging news in the form of a crash course on how to have a growth mind-set. Those who were getting the worst grades before taking the course saw significant improvements in their GPAs later that year. Not only that, but all students who'd been randomly assigned to take the growth mind-set course were more likely to enroll in advanced mathematics classes, regardless of their past academic performance. Students who wouldn't otherwise have had the confidence to try were grappling with complex algebra and geometry, trigonometry and precalculus, opening themselves up to a host of opportunities thanks to their new understanding of the best response to setbacks.

Thankfully, it's not just students who can learn to reinterpret failure in a positive light. Developing a growth mind-set has proven valuable in a host of other environments, ranging from helping students make better hypothetical business decisions to prompting Israelis and Palestinians to see one another and the prospects of resolving their conflicts more productively.

A related line of research, initiated by the Stanford psychologist Claude Steele in the 1980s, has shown that engaging in self-affirmation—focusing on personal experiences that make us feel successful or proud—can improve our resilience in response to threats. Self-affirmation exercises can even improve the decision quality of stigmatized groups.*

When we're pursuing a big goal, disappointment is inevitable. And when we get discouraged, it can be tempting to give up. So it's critical to allow for mistakes and prevent them from sullying a strong performance streak. By preparing to recover from the occasional failure and focusing on past successes, we can conquer self-doubt, build resilience, and make it easier to change for years to come—not just until we hit the first bump in the road.

---

*For instance, research has shown that the poor are stigmatized as incompetent and widely disrespected, which can lead to diminished cognitive performance. Self-affirmation can help reduce these disadvantages (Susan Fiske, *Envy Up, Scorn Down: How Status Divides Us* [New York: Russell Sage Foundation, 2011]; H. R. Kerbo, "The Stigma of Welfare and a Passive Poor," *Sociology and Social Research* 60, no. 2 [1976]: 173–187; A. Mani et al., "Poverty Impedes Cognitive Function," *Science* 341, no. 6149 [2013]: 976–80, DOI:10.1126/science.1238041; and Crystal C. Hall, Jiaying Zhao, and Eldar Shafir, "Self-Affirmation Among the Poor: Cognitive and Behavioral Implications," *Psychological Science* 25, no. 2 [2013]: 619–25, DOI:10.1177/0956797613510949).

THE IMPORTANCE OF CONFIDENCE

Behavioral science buffs might find it peculiar that I've devoted an entire chapter of this book to building confidence. After all, our tendency as a species toward overconfidence—or believing we're more capable, intelligent, and well calibrated than we are—is frequently lamented as one of the most robust and problematic of all human biases. I've even complained about it in this book! Daniel Kahneman, the Nobel laureate who is often called the cofounder of behavioral economics, famously declared overconfidence to be the bias he would most like to eliminate if he could eradicate just one with a stroke of magic.

However, as problematic as overconfidence can be, researchers suspect that so many of us are overconfident because believing in yourself is *absolutely* critical when you pursue ambitious goals. Evolutionarily speaking, a little excess confidence may, on average, produce better results. When interviewing two job candidates who have identical résumés, both pointing toward average skills, would you be more likely to hire the person who conveys that they expect to be average or the candidate who says they expect to excel? The answer is obvious. We all want the person who exudes confidence. While that may not always be the savviest choice (no one wants to end up with an obnoxiously cocky coworker), I suspect we feel comfortable hiring a person who radiates confidence in part because it suggests they'll keep getting up in the face of failure.

But where *excess* confidence can help as well as hurt goal strivers, *under*confidence can only stymie their success, so it's critical to address. Because the signals we receive from the people around us shape our beliefs about what's possible, we should take care to surround ourselves with people who will buoy our own beliefs in our potential and support our growth. And when hoping to help others change, we need to provide that same kind of supportive and encouraging mentorship.

Lauren Eskreis-Winkler's work shows that we can undermine people's chances of success by offering them unsolicited advice (which implies we don't think they have what it takes) and that we can boost their likelihood of achievement by asking for their own advice (which conveys confidence and trust in them and their abilities). And when pursuing your own goals, Lauren's work suggests just how much it can help to put yourself in the position of an adviser.

But there are other ways, besides giving or asking for advice, that we imply judgment about others. Any time we act on negative stereotypes, like asking a man to run the numbers and a woman to take notes in a meeting (implying "men are better at math" and "women are better at office housework"), we send messages about who has what it takes to succeed.

Research has also shown that even the way we compliment people can boost or break their self-confidence. When someone is praised for a "natural" talent, they may develop a fixed mind-set, interpreting failures as a reflection of who they are and accepting defeat. On the other hand, someone who has been praised for their hard work will recognize that effort yields results. So don't say, "That was a brilliant presentation," the next time your employee nails a sales pitch. Instead, say, "I'm wowed by the way your pitches just keep improving."

Because these small signals make a big difference, it's crucial to remember that confidence is key when we're pursuing change. No one can make a major breakthrough without experiencing setbacks along the way—the decisive factor is how we respond. By surrounding ourselves with supporters, putting ourselves in the position of advice givers, letting ourselves off the hook for small failures, and recognizing that setbacks help us grow, we can overcome self-doubt. As the saying goes, "Believe you can, and you're halfway there."

Chapter Takeaways

- Self-doubt can keep you from making progress on your goals or prevent you from setting goals in the first place.

- Giving people unsolicited advice can undermine their confidence. But asking them to give advice builds confidence and helps them think through strategies for achieving their goals. Giving advice can also help us act, because it can feel hypocritical not to do the things we advise other people to do.

- Consider forming advice clubs with friends or colleagues attempting to achieve similar goals or consider becoming a mentor to someone. By giving (solicited) feedback to others, you can boost your confidence and unearth helpful ideas for making progress in your own life.

- Your expectations shape your reality. So, convey to people that you believe in their potential, and surround yourself with mentors who send those same positive signals to you.

- Set ambitious goals (say, exercising every day) but allow yourself a limited number of emergency passes when you slip up (say, two per week). That strategy can help you stay confident and on track even when you face the occasional, inevitable setback.

- Adopting a "growth mind-set"—recognizing that abilities, including intelligence, are not fixed and that effort influences a person's potential—can help you bounce back from setbacks. You can also teach other people to adopt a growth mind-set.

- Focus on personal experiences that make you feel successful or proud. This kind of self-affirmation makes you more resilient and helps you quash self-doubt.

CHAPTER 7

Conformity

Like most college freshmen, Scott Carrell felt anxious when he arrived at the U.S. Air Force Academy's sprawling Colorado campus in the summer of 1991. He'd been a stellar student in high school and hoped he'd shine here, too, but he wasn't sure he had what it takes to excel at one of the most rigorous military academies in the world.

Still, Scott felt he had a leg up on other first-year cadets (called "doolies") because he'd have his identical twin to help him through tough moments. He envisioned the two of them pushing each other on the athletic fields, making friends together, and preparing each other for the academy's notoriously difficult classes. But those dreams were quickly dashed. Moments after arriving on campus, Scott and his brother, Rich, were assigned to separate squadrons of thirty students with whom they would live, eat, exercise, and study throughout their freshman year.

Because it's forbidden for doolies to enter the premises of other squadrons or to leave their own for anything other than classes or athletics, Scott rarely got to see his brother and instead found himself confined to the isolated social bubble to which he'd been assigned. "If [Rich and I] wanted to talk to each other, we'd have to meet at church on Sunday or coordinate at football practice," Scott told me.

When the Carrells were able to talk—usually during prearranged meetings at the library—Scott received a dose of discouragement. Although he'd been the better student in high school, he was startled to learn that his twin was suddenly outperforming him academically. "They wanted him to be a physics major," Scott said. "I thought, 'How is this possible? I'm smarter than my brother.'"

Scott did just fine in the end—well enough to earn a spot in an economics PhD program. But years later, as an economist studying what drives academic achievement, he found himself thinking back to his twin's first-year stardom, wondering about the impact of the people picked to surround him. He'd started reading economics and psychology research about the impact peer groups can have on people's decisions, and he wondered if his academy peers might hold the answer, particularly given the strength of squadron bonds.

WHY WE SOAK UP SOCIAL NORMS

One day every February, the packed lecture hall where I teach my Wharton MBAs erupts with the cheers of enthusiastic twentysomethings. Full-grown men and women leap from their seats, hooting and hollering like they're at Mardi Gras. I always wonder if campus security will show up, worried something is wrong.

But nothing is wrong. My students are responding exactly how I asked them to in an email sent the night before. Each year, I reach out to all but three people enrolled in my class announcing that at the start of the next day's lecture, I'll show a picture of our school's dean in my slideshow. The email provides clear instructions. When they see the photo, I want them to applaud enthusiastically. But not everyone in the class is getting this message, I explain, so please don't forward or discuss it. The plan is to see how the three students I've left off my e-list will react when the rest of the room claps for the dean. Will they watch in bewilderment? Or will they join in?

You can probably guess what happens. Although there's some variation from year to year, most of my guinea pigs wait a beat and then enthusiastically begin to clap, following their classmates' lead.

Like any well-prepared instructor, I've carefully noted where my "special" students are seated, and after the room quiets, I call on one of them.

"Could you tell us why you were clapping?" I ask. The responses, which come after a moment of wide-eyed hesitation (it's nerve-racking to be singled out), are almost as reliable as the prearranged applause. "I just clapped because everyone else did," my students typically answer, hoping I'll accept this explanation and move on.

I don't. Instead, I push them to think about how they'd feel if they walked into a party in jeans only to find everyone else decked out in formalwear. "Deeply uncomfortable," "humiliated," and "mortified" are some of the most common answers. The responses highlight the first reason students left off my warning email start clapping when their peers burst into applause: We feel like misfits when we stand out from the crowd.

I then ask my students a second question: "Imagine you're in an auditorium and you see a crowd rushing for the fire exit. What's the right thing to do?" The answer is unanimous: Follow them! This time, though, the logic behind the herd behavior is different. No one is worried about fitting in. Rather, we suspect other people have noticed something dangerous that we missed. Sometimes, other peoples' decisions reflect valuable information (in this case, it would be about a threat; in the case of my clapping experiment, it would be about school news the students might have missed).

Consciously or subconsciously, norms create pressure to conform so we won't experience social discomfort or sanctions but can instead enjoy "fitting in"; and they often also convey information about how to acquire "payoffs" that we might otherwise overlook (such as avoiding a threat).

When he learned about research on these very laws of social influence, UC Davis economist Scott Carrell wondered if they could help explain why his twin brother had suddenly surpassed him, academically, in their early days as cadets at the U.S. Air Force Academy.

Now a frequent guest lecturer at the academy, Scott knew just how critical squadron assignments were to the lives of doolies—a squadron becomes a cadet's entire social universe. He also knew that in spite of their importance, squadrons were assigned by random lottery. This meant that his alma mater had unintentionally created a natural experiment on social influence.

Curious if this might solve the riddle from his doolie days, Scott was inspired to study how those *randomly assigned* to surround any one cadet might affect them. Could rubbing elbows with hotshots have lifted his brother's grades? Scott's knowledge of past research on the power of social influence led him to suspect that the academic performance of squadron mates might affect a doolie's grades much the same way my MBAs influence their peers in my clapping experiment. First, if everyone in your squadron is studying hard and earning good grades, you'll feel like a misfit if you don't hit the books and get some As yourself. And second, you may realize your fellow cadets have figured out that goofing off comes with negative consequences.

To test his hunch about peer influence, Scott crunched the numbers with a team of collaborators, analyzing three years of academic data on roughly thirty-five hundred doolies who'd been randomly assigned to their academy squadrons.* He found that for every 100-point increase in the average verbal SAT score of a doolie's squadron cohort, that cadet's first-year GPA rose by 0.4 grade points on a 4.0 scale. That's the difference between getting all A minuses and being a B or B plus student. The luck of the draw seemed to have a real impact on who got off to a roaring start at the academy and who didn't. Perhaps it could explain his twin's early success.

Scott's findings show just how important it is to be in good company when you hope to achieve big goals and how harmful it can be to have peers who aren't high achievers. A growing body of evidence suggests that the people you've spent time with have been shaping your behavior your whole life, often without your knowledge. For instance, one study showed that when your peers attend a retirement savings workshop, there are spillover effects—not only do their savings increase, but you're also more likely to save for your golden years, even if you never attended a workshop yourself. Your mom was onto something when she told you to stop hanging around with bad apples and find some good ones. Everything from our grades to our careers to our financial decisions is shaped, at least in part, by our peers.

In the summer of 2006, Scott got a call from the Air Force Academy's top brass. As a loyal alumnus who visited each summer on reserve

---

*Verbal SAT scores were used as a proxy for academic quality.

duty to teach a class and offer consulting services, he was used to getting inquiries from leadership. But this time the voice on the other side of the line was unusually urgent.

First-year cadets were struggling. Grades were down and the dropout rate was up, but no one could determine why or what to do about it. Could Scott help?

COPY AND PASTE

Although the Air Force Academy fosters an unusually strong environment for bonding, college is an important time of social imprinting for students everywhere. Like many coeds, when she was a junior at Syracuse University, my friend Kassie Brabaw experienced this firsthand when she signed up to work as a resident adviser to save on expenses. Being an RA allowed her to live in a dorm for free, as long as she made herself available to freshmen in need of guidance on everything from managing classwork to roommate squabbles to living away from home for the first time. To become an RA, Kassie had to spend a week in all-day training sessions with a dozen other upperclassmen who would be responsible for their own flocks of incoming freshmen.

As luck would have it, five of Kassie's fellow RAs-to-be were vegetarians. She'd long been intrigued by the idea of a meatless lifestyle—it seemed healthy and virtuous. But she never really believed she could do it. Her family ate meat at every meal and rarely bought fresh vegetables. So even though vegetarianism sounded great, she had no idea what vegetarians actually ate. Was it just salads, salads, and more salads? That was what she imagined and it sounded boring.

But as the week went by, Kassie watched, amazed, as her vegetarian peers created delicious-looking meals at campus dining halls. Their diets were light on lettuce and heavy on variety—loaded veggie omelets every morning, black bean soup or vegetarian risotto for lunch. And when her RA group went out for a meal, she was delighted to discover that ordering at restaurants was a breeze. "All they had to ask was, 'Is there chicken stock in this soup?'" she told me.

When training was over, Kassie realized she could easily emulate the strategies that had worked so well for the vegetarians in her RA cohort: eating tasty omelets for breakfast, soups and risottos for lunch, and so on. She decided to try a meatless life for a week. That week then turned into a month, which turned into four years. Although she didn't have a name for it, Kassie had used a strategy I use myself when I want to master a new skill: "copy and paste." She watched peers who had managed to achieve a goal she wanted to achieve and then deliberately imitated their methods.

My frequent collaborator, Angela Duckworth, and I often take the same approach. I've copied and pasted her strategy of handling work calls while she walks to the office, and she's emulated my practice of drafting emails from preexisting templates.

In mentoring students, though, we've both been surprised by how often a simple suggestion—"Did you think about asking your friend who's acing this class how she studies?"—leads to a blank stare. Of course, we know that *some* copying and pasting occurs naturally. My MBA students copy their clapping classmates. And when Kassie lived in close quarters with vegetarians, she realized she could and should imitate their approach if she wanted to change her diet. But Angela and I suspected that many people never wake up to the opportunity to deliberately emulate their peers. After all, while Kassie was thrown together with some vegetarians for a week and it changed her life, it had never previously occurred to her to go *looking* for them.

This may well be thanks to something social psychologists Lee Ross, David Greene, and Pamela House first pointed out in 1977 in a now famous paper on what they dubbed the "false consensus effect." The paper describes a general tendency humans have to incorrectly assume that other people see and react to the world the same way we do. If we think the latest juice cleanse being promoted on morning talk shows is inane, we assume most other people do, too; if we think urban life is ideal, we assume that like us, the majority of our fellow countrymen aspire to move to cities; and if we're clueless about how to make tasty vegetarian meals, we assume other people (even vegetarians!) are equally uninformed. Of course, the real world is far more diverse than the world in our imaginations, and wide differences in beliefs, behaviors, and knowledge exist in objective reality.

A few years ago, Angela and I began to wonder if more people could reach their goals if they were encouraged to (1) seek out people with a wealth of knowledge they'd likely overlooked, and (2) deliberately copy and paste their life hacks. If we generally underappreciate how much we can learn from other people because we assume we already know everything they do, maybe we could use a little prompting to make better use of our social connections.

In two studies led by Wharton doctoral student Katie Mehr, we found that encouraging people to copy and paste one another's best life hacks motivated both more exercise and better class preparation in adults who wanted to work out more and college students seeking to improve their grades, respectively. Score one small victory for the strategy.

Our next study was more ambitious, and more complicated. More than one thousand participants hoping to boost their exercise regimens were randomly assigned to one of three groups: a control group in which they were simply encouraged to plan how they would increase their activity, an experimental group in which they made plans but were also encouraged to use our "copy and paste" strategy, or a second experimental group in which they made plans and were given a workout hack to copy that was obtained by someone else (like "for every hour that you exercise, allow yourself fifteen minutes on social media").

Consistent with our prior findings, we saw that having any new exercise-boosting technique to copy worked better than just making a plan, regardless of where the technique came from. But interestingly, it was more helpful if people found strategies to copy and paste *themselves* than if the strategies came from someone else. When we dug into the data, we discovered that seeking out exercise hacks to copy and paste led people to find tips that best fit their own lifestyles. What's more, taking a more active approach to information gathering increased the time participants spent with their role models, increasing their exposure to good habits. Together, these findings confirmed our suspicion about what people stand to gain from *deliberately* copying the successful strategies used by peers. So if you want to get fit, tip books will surely help, but if you can spend some time with fit peers and watch out for ideas, you'll likely do even better.

When we're unsure of ourselves, a powerful way the people around us can help boost our capacity and confidence is by showing us what's possible. Often, in fact, we're more influenced by observation than by advice. By watching her vegetarian peers create meals in the dining hall and order in restaurants, Kassie was able to pick up techniques that made vegetarianism work for her. Similarly, Air

Force Academy doolies whose grades improved thanks to studious squadron mates surely felt pressure to measure up to their peers. And when that pressure built, at least some likely noticed study strategies they could mimic. But my recent research suggests that if cadets *deliberately* looked to "copy and paste" successful tips, they could benefit even more. After all, if we were naturally squeezing all the insights we could out of our peers, nudges to copy and paste wouldn't be of any use.

Happily, it's easy to turn yourself into a deliberate copy-and-paster. The next time you're falling short of a goal, look to high-achieving peers for answers. If you'd like to get more sleep, a well-rested friend with a similar lifestyle may be able to help. If you'd like to commute on public transit, don't just look up the train schedules—talk to a neighbor who's already abandoned her car. You're likely to go further faster if you find the person who's already achieving what you want to achieve and copy and paste their tactics than if you simply let social forces influence you through osmosis.

INFLUENCING OTHER PEOPLE WITH SOCIAL NORMS

If you ever stay at hotels, you've probably encountered signs in the bathroom urging you to reuse your towels to help save water. But if you're like me, you balked the first time you saw this request. Who knows how many kinds of flesh-eating mold might grow in a heavily trafficked hotel bathroom? (The truth: basically none, but my mind goes there.)

Recognizing that the idea of reusing towels might sound peculiar to some guests, psychologists Noah Goldstein, Bob Cialdini, and Vladas Griskevicius partnered with a hotel to persuade more guests to make the green choice. They suspected social influence could be used in their favor—after all, if people thought reusing towels sounded weird, how better to normalize it than by clarifying that it was, in fact, normal? But the researchers had a problem. Hotel guests can't see what other guests are up to when it comes to towel use (hurrah for private showers!). To address this, they decided to try simply *describing* what was normal. In theory, at least, social norms should shape behavior even when people merely read about what their peers are doing, rather than watching them in the act. But the theory needed a test.

The old signs in hotel bathrooms were swapped out for new ones, which boldly proclaimed: "Join your fellow guests in helping to save the environment," and shared the news that 75 percent of guests typically use their towels more than once. The results were encouraging— the new signs generated an 18 percent increase in towel reuse. But even more impressively, a tweak to the message nearly doubled its impact. When patrons were told that most guests who stayed in their *very room* reused their towels, 33 percent more people chose to do the same. This, I think, is the most interesting finding from the study. It suggests we're particularly eager to emulate people whose circumstances resemble our own, even in superficial ways.

A get-out-the-vote experiment on Facebook offers more evidence of this tendency. In an attempt to increase turnout, the world's largest social network told randomly selected U.S. users that many of their friends had already voted in the 2010 midterms and showed up to six pictures of those friends. While seeing any friend made a user more likely to show up at the polls, when *close* friends were depicted, the effects were up to four times larger.

These studies highlight that the closer we are to someone and the more their situation resembles our own, the more likely we are to be influenced by their behavior, even if the behavior is merely described rather than directly observed.* They also speak to the power of using norms as a tool of influence. Describing what's typical can be an effective way to help large groups change their behaviors for the better.

But we should keep in mind the serious ethical quandaries that come with this tactic. Much of the early research on the sway of social norms was motivated by scientists' desire to understand how the Nazis could have compelled the complicity of ordinary Germans in the Holocaust. Findings that followed have proven that social pressure can be used to persuade us to do seriously immoral things, which should rightfully give you pause. It's important to beware of social pressure's potentially coercive power.

After explaining the influence of social norms, I always remind my MBAs of what they've heard before. Most of us have known since childhood that "everyone else is doing it" isn't a good excuse for bad behavior. But in spite of this, social pressure can still have a toxic influence. The good news is that there are ways to weaken its choke hold: coercive uses of social pressure tend to be less effective when we aren't face-to-face with the person pressuring us to act, when we

---

*The value of describing norms to encourage behavior change—a technique called "social norms marketing"—has now been well established, with research proving it can shape everything from towel reuse to tax payments (Organisation for Economic Co-operation and Development [OECD], "Behavioural Insights and Public Policy: Lessons from around the World" [Paris: OECD Publishing, 2017], DOI:10.1787/978926 4270480-en).

have a chance to reflect, and when we can consider our intended actions with a fellow skeptic. And so, before jumping on any bandwagon to do something that feels at all uncomfortable, imprudent, or unethical, I encourage slowing down, dodging in-person interactions with whoever's applying pressure, and talking with a devil's advocate (or in this case, an angel's advocate) to improve decisions.

While social influence tactics can unquestionably be used for nefarious purposes, they needn't be a force for evil, thankfully, and often aren't. When harnessed to help people, social norms can play a valuable role in changing our behavior for the better. Scott Carrell had just that vision when he learned Air Force Academy doolies were struggling academically and that he might get a chance to help.

WHEN POSITIVE SOCIAL
NORMS BACKFIRE

When Scott received that urgent call from academy leadership about the plummeting grades of first-year cadets, he thought back to his study showing the influence of squadron assignments on doolie performance. After hanging up the phone, he sat down and wrote a detailed plan.

Instead of creating squadron assignments randomly, Scott told the academy's leadership that they should deliberately group the worst performers on the verbal SATs with the best.* The influence of the

---

*Note that Scott's number crunching pointed to a new, tougher chemistry textbook as the most likely culprit for the recent drop in doolie grades. But since it was now ensconced in the academy curriculum, he saw his idea as the best way to buck a downward trend in first-year cadets' academic performance.

stronger students will bring up the grades of their squadron mates, he reasoned, and the project will cost nothing to boot.

With a promise like that, it's no wonder that the top brass quickly gave Scott and his team the green light to move forward with their plan, authorizing an experimental approach so that Scott would be able to prove the value of his handiwork. Presumably, other universities around the world could then build on this success.

In 2007 and 2008, under the meticulous direction of Scott's team, academy administrators placed some low-performing students in squadrons with high-performing students and crossed their fingers that the top performers' study habits would rub off. (Middling students were left in groups with other middling students.) To provide a point of comparison, another set of squadron assignments was made the old-fashioned way—randomly. At the end of the experiment, Scott and his collaborators assessed the academic performance of cadets across the two groups.

Scott was so sure of what he would find that he drafted the introduction to a paper describing his expected results before any data came back. He couldn't wait to share his success story, giving schools around the world the chance to benefit from the academy's innovation. So when he first ran the numbers on cadet grades, he was bewildered. There must be some mistake, he thought, as he placed a call to his data source. "Did you accidentally switch the treatment and control groups?" he asked.

But the error was in Scott's predictions. After a thorough review of the data, the dismal numbers were confirmed. For two years in a row, the new squadron-assignment algorithm had been *harming* doolies' grades, not helping them—doolies in carefully selected squadrons were doing worse in school than cadets who had been randomly assigned to their peer groups following the usual protocols. *Oh crap!* thought Scott, as he made frantic calls to ensure that the new squadron-assignment system would be scrapped before the next class of doolies arrived.

But ending the experiment was only his first responsibility—his second was to understand *why* it had backfired. Scott started surveying students and crunching more numbers to make sense of his results. Pretty quickly, the problem became clear. Instead of intermingling and influencing one another as the researchers expected, the students in squadrons of high and low performers had segregated themselves. With no middle performers to build a social bridge between cadets at the extremes, the squadrons became polarized, and struggling students suffered. Scott had unwittingly demonstrated a serious weakness in what many viewed as a tried and true influence tactic.

Imagine a social universe in which your colleagues, classmates, and neighbors are constantly outstripping you. Day after day, you discover that you earned less, ran slower, tested worse, and generally paled in comparison to your superstar peers. Sounds kind of awful, right? You might sink into hopelessness and start to steer clear of the overachievers. It'd be comforting to call the situation that Scott had uncovered extraordinary and just move on, but evidence has taught me otherwise.*

My lesson came when I teamed up with a group of economists to help a large U.S. manufacturing company boost its employees' retirement savings. Happily, most of the workers were already saving at a high rate, but there were still thousands of low savers and nonsavers

---

*It's worth noting that rising inequality means that this is a situation many marginalized groups find themselves in far too often.

to worry about. Many had never actively declined to save, they just hadn't opted in to the company's retirement savings program. And these people seemed to us like good targets for a little social pressure. If they thought saving sounded too hard, we figured we could disabuse them of that idea by letting them know how many of their co-workers were managing to do it. Maybe our message would also generate some healthy guilt and competition.

But like Scott's scheme, our plan backfired. In fact, it was a double whammy. First, just letting employees know that most of their colleagues were saving *depressed* sign-up rates for the company's retirement program. Second, when we experimentally ratcheted up the reported fraction of savers in an employee's age group from 77 percent to 92 percent (by randomizing the width of the age bracket used for comparisons*), sign-ups trended downward. That is, the stronger the social norm we conveyed, the worse things got. While our results were a bit harder to explain than Scott's, our best bet, based on follow-up research, is this: A suitable retirement nest egg is something you accumulate over time. It takes patience—you can't catch up with the Joneses in a matter of weeks. As a result, comparisons with disciplined savers might be exactly the *wrong* message for people who are already worried they're falling behind. Our mailings likely depressed people's hopes further—we made them feel as if they could never catch up! Our results made us think about the "what-the-hell effect" I've described before. If you're going to fail, research shows people often feel they might as well do it with a bang.

---

*We were able to experimentally change the numbers we showed people without lying by randomizing which age bucket we put each employee into when making social comparisons (e.g., others aged 40 to 50 versus 40 to 45). My frequent collaborator, John Beshears, deserves all the credit for this clever design.

Consistent with this idea, we saw that the lowest relative earners exhibited the strongest backlash when they learned how many other people were saving for retirement.

This study and the failure of the Air Force Academy's attempts at social engineering offer an important lesson. For social influence to work, there can't be too stark a difference between overachievers and those in need of a boost. If you're hoping to become a faster swimmer, don't start practicing next to Olympic gold medalist Katie Ledecky. Even if you thought to copy and paste her routines, you might sense, correctly, that the limits of your natural talent would interfere with the benefits of having insight into her training regimen.

Similarly, my team's work on retirement savings suggests that describing others' accomplishments is an effective motivator only when their achievements feel like something we can emulate fairly quickly. Some goals require a simple change, but many are more complicated and take a major, extended commitment. If you want to go green, it's possible to change your energy-use habits in a month and become an efficiency champion. If you want to be more active, you can change your daily step count in, well, a day. But you can't hit a 401(k) goal overnight. In endeavors that require sustained effort, finding out that we're *way* behind our peers can break our spirit.

Social influence tactics can add far more value when the focus is on concrete, immediately achievable goals, such as voting or spending fewer hours on social media rather than more long-term or abstract goals, like saving more for retirement. Luckily, there's a way to make long-term goals feel more achievable in the short term. In the third chapter of this book I shared research on the importance of breaking big goals into smaller subcomponents—say, encouraging people to save 5 dollars a day instead of 150 dollars a month or to volunteer four hours a week instead of two hundred hours a year. Breaking down big goals can help bridge the gap between what sounds doable and what sounds impossibly out of reach, potentially preventing social influence tactics from backfiring. And encouraging small, concrete changes can make a big difference in the long run, as repeated social norms messaging has been proven to change behavior not once, twice, or three times, but for years and years on end.

HE SEES YOU WHEN YOU'RE SLEEPING

Perhaps one of the most fraught features of social norms showed up in my classroom clapping experiment. And that's the pressure that norms create to change your behavior because you realize you're being watched and judged. While that pressure may sound quite harmful—and it can be—it also has the potential to drive positive behavior change.

To understand how feeling watched alters our behavior, consider what happened one day in 2006 when twenty thousand Michigan residents found a strange letter in the mail.

At first glance, these letters just looked like another plea from political canvassers to vote in an upcoming primary election. But on closer inspection, they were surprisingly personal. Each recipient saw a list of the recent elections they'd voted in and those they'd skipped, along with a report on the turnout decisions of each of their neighbors. Not only did the letters display personal voting records, they promised to release updated data to everyone in the community right after Election Day. The message? Vote or be outed to your neighbors as a bad citizen.

You might wonder what politician would be zany enough to send such an aggressive mailing, and your skepticism would be warranted. But this message didn't come from a candidate for office—it was part of an experiment by political scientists Alan Gerber, Donald Green, and Christopher Larimer testing inexpensive strategies for boosting voter turnout.

The researchers compiled more than 180,000 addresses from publicly available lists of qualified state voters and drafted four different mailings to remind people about the upcoming election. Some prospective voters received no mailings, and others received boilerplate voting reminders. These groups were included in the study to provide a baseline for comparison. The remaining households were subjected to varying degrees of social pressure to turn out on Election Day. The mailing that revealed the voting histories of everyone in a given neighborhood was the most extreme. Another mailing listed the voting histories of everyone who lived in the same house, while a third simply explained that researchers were running a study and would check if you'd voted.

When I first heard about this experiment, I had a moment of disbelief, since it felt very Big Brother to me. But before we talk about the moral dubiousness of subjecting people to public shaming, let me tell you how this social pressure campaign worked. Because the results were astounding.

The simple reminder increased turnout by almost 2 percentage points (which is a big deal in a low turnout or close election), while the mailings about tracking led to a boost of 2.6 percentage points. But the action really started to happen when people expected to be held accountable to someone they knew. Among those who were warned that everyone they lived with would find out whether or not they'd voted, turnout increased by 4.9 percentage points. And when the idea of being reported on to their neighbors was introduced, things got truly extreme. The mailing that promised to reveal voting records to everyone on the block produced an 8.1 percentage point increase in turnout. To my knowledge, no other junk mail campaign has ever generated nearly as large an increase in voting.

This form of social accountability and its potency may sound quite familiar to you if, in the days leading up to Christmas, you've used the legendary omniscience of Santa Claus to motivate good behavior in your children (or if your parents used this tactic on you). As crooners from Bing Crosby to Frank Sinatra to Mariah Carey have cautioned us, "He knows if you've been bad or good, so be good for goodness sake!" At least in my household, the threat that Santa is watching and may withhold gifts if he doesn't like what he sees works wonders. My son is always on his best behavior in December. But the disciplinary tactics parents use with their children are often ill-suited for settings with less asymmetric power structures. Which brings me back to the disbelief I felt when I first learned about this study.

It turns out, my concern was well warranted. While highly effective, the experiment generated serious blowback (one reporter supposedly camped out for days at the PO Box listed on the mailings' return address to ambush whoever was responsible for sending them), which helps explain why you likely haven't received a similar letter.

But in spite of its shortcomings, I find this study fascinating because it proves so resoundingly that creating social accountability can dramatically change our behavior. You can easily use it to help yourself by turning social accountability into a commitment device. For example, if you tell your coworkers you plan to take your Certified Public Accountant Examination this spring and make sure they'll find out if you don't, you'll get the benefits of accountability with no risk of backlash. You could also ask a friend to be your gym buddy, so you'll both be held accountable for skipping a workout. This has the added benefit of making workouts more fun.*

Still, if you want to use accountability as an overt tool to spur others toward their goals, you should keep in mind the anger that such tactics can create. Threatening to expose someone to the scrutiny of others may quickly make you an enemy, for good reason. That said, with a little attention to detail, social pressure *can* be used inoffensively. A 2013 experiment in California makes the case.

The goal was to boost sign-ups for a green energy initiative that required homeowners to accept service outages on days when energy demand was at its peak. (Translation: hot days when everyone is blasting their air-conditioning.) This was a challenge for obvious reasons, but the research team had a clever plan. In some communities, rather than sharing homeowners' sign-up decisions with their neighbors, the researchers let the homeowners themselves spread the word, setting up public bulletin boards so that anyone could see who had (or hadn't) signed up. In other neighborhoods, the bulletin boards allowed sign-ups only under anonymous ID numbers (so neighbors would know how many people had signed up before them, but not who).

Stark differences emerged. When people signed up by name on a public bulletin board, the popularity of the green energy program tripled. But most important, there was no blowback here: because enrollment was optional, it didn't feel like being outed; if anything, signing

---

*My collaborators and I have proven that paying people 1 dollar for every gym visit made in sync with a friend boosts exercise 37 percent more than paying people 1 dollar for every gym visit made unconditionally. The payments linked to joint workouts boosted accountability and enjoyment (Rachel Gershon, Cynthia Cryder, and Katherine L. Milkman, "Friends with Health Benefits: A Field Experiment" [working paper, 2021]).

up publicly probably felt to some like a chance to brag. The psychology is similar—it's all about public accountability—but people react totally differently when disclosure feels like a chance to show off.*

Most of us want to look like good, hardworking, successful people to our friends, neighbors, and colleagues. So when our actions are visible, there's a strong pull to do the "right" thing and a strong deterrent from making the "wrong" choice, which stands to tarnish our good reputations. To successfully harness those instincts without creating blowback, it's best to allow people the chance to earn praise or opt out.

Overall, it's clear that if you're hoping to encourage others to adopt better behaviors, you can use humans' love of adulation to your advantage. For instance, research has shown that when our charitable gifts will be announced to others, we're more likely to make donations. So if you're fundraising, find a way to let people broadcast their generosity. And if you're hoping to get more employees to participate in workplace training or mentoring programs, consider posting public sign-up lists. Social pressure to do the "right" thing will build, and as the list grows, social norms will also work in your favor—it will become clear that signing up is *cool*.

---

*When someone tells on us for misbehavior, it's what scientists call an act of "commission"; but when they fail to draw attention to our good behavior, it's an "omission." And research shows omissions offend us far less than commissions (think about how bad it feels when someone reprimands you versus when they simply fail to draw attention to your excellence). When researchers posted public sign-ups for a green energy program (typically considered a good behavior, at least in California), the accountability they created came in the form of an omission. Those who didn't sign up missed a chance for public praise, but because neighbors had to infer from the fact that a name wasn't on a list that someone didn't sign up, the reprimand for failure to go green wasn't overt. Explicitly outing nonvoters to their neighbors, on the other hand, is an act of commission, and thus infuriated many (Mark Spranca, Elisa Minsk, and Jonathan Baron, "Omission and Commission in Judgment and Choice," *Journal of Experimental Social Psychology* 27, no. 1 [1991]: 76–105, DOI:10.1016/0022-1031(91)90011-T).

USING SOCIAL FORCES FOR GOOD

Social forces can be powerful drivers of behavior change, helping us overcome self-doubt by highlighting what lots of others in the same position have managed to do. But what if a good behavior isn't all that popular? What if most people in your workplace aren't recycling, mentoring their peers, adhering to safety protocols, or doing whatever it is you'd like to help them (and yourself) do more consistently?

All hope is not lost. Studies have shown that if a behavior is merely trending upward, rather than widely popular, sharing information about that trend can win people over.* If you find out that just 20 percent of your colleagues are enrolled in a new computer programming boot camp, you might hesitate, but if you discover that enrollment has doubled since last year, you'll have a different perspective. An upward trend tells people that this counternormative behavior will eventually become the thing "everyone" is doing.

While I've focused on how to help other people achieve their goals with social forces, this strategy is also a powerful tool to use on yourself. If you're planning to run a marathon, try to train alongside people who know what it's like to cross the finish line. Schedule running sessions with them and connect on Fitbit so that they can see your

---

*In one study, hundreds of patrons at a café were assigned to one of three groups. Some were told that 30 percent of Americans make an effort to limit their meat consumption. Others learned that 30 percent of Americans had *begun* limiting their meat consumption in the last five years (indicating an upward trend). A final group was given no information about meat-eating norms in America. Patrons told about the upward trend in meat avoidance were twice as likely as those given no information about meat eating to order a vegetarian lunch. And the trend information also worked far better than sharing the static norm that most people *don't* limit meat consumption (Gregg Sparkman and Gregory M. Walton, "Dynamic Norms Promote Sustainable Behavior, Even If It Is Counternormative," *Psychological Science* 28, no. 11 [2017]: 1663–74, DOI:10.1177/0956797617719950).

stats and chide you if you have a slow week. And be sure to ask for guidance so that you can copy and paste what's worked for them.

This isn't rocket science, but it does seem to be an underappreciated science. Knowingly or not, many of us benefit from social forces. Ask Kassie, who copied her friends' eating habits to become a successful vegetarian, or Scott, who learned just how much Air Force Academy doolies' high-achieving peers unknowingly influence their study habits. If you channel the power of social forces correctly, you can boost capacity and self-confidence and achieve more while showing colleagues and friends how to do the same.

Chapter Takeaways

- When you're facing self-doubt or uncertainty about how to proceed, a powerful way the people around you can help boost your capacity and confidence is by showing you what's possible.

- Your decisions are heavily influenced by the norms in your peer group, so it's important to be in good company when you hope to achieve big goals, and it can be harmful to have peers who are low achievers.

- Just describing what behavior is typical (assuming it's a desirable behavior) can be an effective way to help other people change their behaviors for the better.

- The closer you are to someone, and the more their situation resembles your own, the more likely you are to be influenced by their behavior.

- Although some peer influence will rub off on you effortlessly, you can supercharge positive peer effects deliberately. Do this by watching peers who have managed to achieve whatever goal you hope to achieve and then copying and pasting their methods.

- Because you care about gaining peer approval, feeling watched by groups of other people changes your behavior.

- To use peer visibility to promote change without creating blowback, rather than publicly shaming people for undesirable behavior, give them the chance to earn public praise (or opt out).

- If a behavior is merely growing in popularity, rather than an existing norm, sharing information about that upward trend can change others' behavior.

- If the achievements of your peers feel vastly out of reach, witnessing or learning about social norms can discourage you from pursuing change rather than encouraging it.

- Social pressure can be used to coerce people. So, before using social norms to influence friends, family, or coworkers, take your moral responsibility seriously.

- If you notice someone using social pressure on you in a way that makes you nervous, slow down, dodge face-to-face interactions with that person, and talk with a devil's advocate to improve your decisions and avoid becoming a victim of coercion.

CHAPTER 8

Changing for Good

I n late 2018, Angela Duckworth and I had a meeting with our research team about early results from the most ambitious behavior change study either of us had ever launched.

"Would you call this project a success?" a staff scientist asked.

"No way," Angela declared at the same time that I said "Absolutely!"

Everyone laughed.

There was good reason for our disagreement. We'd just run a massive experiment with 24 Hour Fitness, a national gym chain, in an attempt to turn more of their members into regular gym goers. Roughly half of Americans don't exercise enough (even Americans with gym memberships), and we were hopeful that we could find a cheap way to encourage more physical activity.

But our mammoth study hadn't turned out exactly as planned.

Tens of thousands of 24 Hour Fitness members had signed up to participate. Most seemed thrilled to join a free four-week digital program meant to boost their exercise. But what we cared about most wasn't who signed up or how happy they were to be there but rather how well our program worked. And that's where there was room for debate.

I focused on the good news. Many of the more than fifty ideas we'd tested had immediately succeeded by building on principles such as the importance of planning, reminders, fun, social norms, and repeated rewards. At almost zero cost, we'd found lots of creative ways to increase gym attendance while people were in our program.

Sounds like a success, right? That's what I thought.

The bad news came when we looked at what happened after our program ended. Almost none of the ideas we'd tested had staying power. To be fair, our study showed that through repetition and reward, people converted maybe a quarter to a third of the extra gym visits we helped them make over the course of a month into lasting habits. But we'd really wanted to discover a few revolutionary, inexpensive techniques for encouraging exercise that could alter people's behavior for years to come. And we hadn't. Thus Angela's sense that we had failed.

While heartened by our short-term success, I shared Angela's disappointment that we hadn't found more four-week interventions with lasting benefits. We'd carefully diagnosed the most important internal obstacles people face when trying to exercise regularly, such as finding workouts unpleasant, inertia, and forgetting, and we'd tackled many of them directly. So I couldn't understand what went wrong. Stumped, I called my friend Kevin Volpp, a star economist and medical doctor who helped build one of the most successful applied behavioral economics research groups in the world.

I wanted Kevin's perspective. Why did he think we'd been so unsuccessful at making behavior change *stick*?

Kevin offered up some unforgettable words of wisdom: "When we diagnose someone with diabetes, we don't put them on insulin for a month, take them off of it, and expect them to be cured." In medicine, doctors recognize that chronic diseases require a lifetime of treatment. Why do we assume that behavior change is any different?

I felt like slapping myself in the forehead. Once I got it, Kevin's point was so obvious that I was embarrassed I'd needed it spelled out.

Study after study (mine included) has shown that achieving transformative behavior change is more like treating a chronic disease than curing a rash. You can't just slap a little ointment on it and expect it to clear up forever. The internal obstacles that stand in the way of change, which I've described in this book—obstacles such as temptation, forgetfulness, underconfidence, and laziness—are like the symptoms of a chronic disease. They won't just go away once you've started "treating" them. They're human nature and require constant vigilance.

One experiment that illustrates this particularly well involved tens of thousands of households that received home-energy reports from an organization called Opower. In monthly or quarterly reports, Opower tells energy-inefficient homeowners how much energy they've used in comparison to their neighbors. Thinking back to the influence of social norms, it shouldn't be surprising to learn that Opower has compelled millions of energy-guzzling customers to conserve power at an amazingly low cost simply by making them aware that they're out of line with neighborhood norms.

The Opower study I find most fascinating, though, compared how patterns of home energy use differed when people stopped getting these reports.

When a randomly selected group was cut off from receiving their home energy updates after two years, they continued to use less energy than households that had never received Opower's mailings. But they didn't conserve as much energy as people who were randomly assigned to *keep* receiving the reports. When cut off after two years of Opower messages, households' conservation efforts decayed by 10 to 20 percent per year. And this was after *two years* of sticking with a new habit. Imagine how much falloff there would have been if they'd gotten the reports only for a month. That's the situation Angela and I encountered.

Like our study with 24 Hour Fitness, this research suggests that the work we do to facilitate behavior change often has enduring positive benefits. But if and when our efforts stop, we should expect to see ourselves and others begin to relapse (and the sooner we stop, the more relapse we should anticipate).

There's a glass-half-full and a glass-half-empty way to look at what happens when efforts to promote change wind down. I prefer the glass-half-full perspective that lasting change is possible. The key is to treat change as a chronic problem, not a temporary one, just as Kevin suggested.

When you use the tools in this book to overcome whatever internal obstacles you face on your journey to create change, recognize that you'll want to use them not once or twice or for a month or for a year or two, but permanently. Or, at least, until you no longer want to achieve whatever it is you set out to achieve in the first place.

Karen Herrera, my student whom you met earlier, knows well that when the barriers to change are internal, the key to success is to tackle them with a tailored suite of solutions and to treat change as a chronic challenge rather than a temporary one. She arrived at college eager to use her fresh start to become a healthier person and successfully developed an approach with a nutritionist that helped her feel happier and healthier than she'd ever been. Years after beginning her journey, she still meets regularly with the same dietician for weigh-ins (which provide accountability), makes plans for healthy meals, schedules workouts on her calendar, tracks calories in an app, and relies on sophisticated strategies for resisting temptations, such as filling up on healthy foods before going to campus events that lure students with free pizza or donuts, preselecting healthy options from online menus before dining out with friends, and satisfying her sweet tooth with fruit smoothies and yogurt that she's come to love. Happily, staying fit has become easier for Karen over time. By consistently relying on a suite of trusted, science-based techniques to overcome obstacles to good health, she's made change stick.

Like Karen, I've found maintaining change in the face of internal obstacles is far easier than initiating it. For many years, I've success-fully engineered change in my own life using the strategies in this book—temptation bundling to make exercise fun so I stay fit, sur-rounding myself with friends and colleagues who believe in me and who are role models to boost my confidence and stretch my ambition, harnessing fresh starts to tackle new challenges (such as writing this book, which I began on the very day I became a homeowner), and making cue-based plans to avoid flaking out.

I've achieved the best results when I've built on what Brad Gilbert taught Andre Agassi—that the key to change is understanding your opponent. One-size-fits-all strategies won't get you nearly as far as tailored attacks on what stands in your way. Once you've mastered that game plan, staying the course is often as simple as sticking to the tactics that have been working for you.

Of course, sometimes the obstacles to change shift. Just as your opponent in tennis can choose to adopt a new strategy midway through a match, forcing you to rethink what had been working, you may need to alter your approach to change from time to time. Students launching their own ventures often come to me struggling to get started or suffering from low self-confidence only to later discover they're on their way and believe they've got what it takes, but that the work has become a chore. If you find you're hitting a wall, revisit the question of what's impeding your progress. You may find that the obstacles have shifted and a new game plan is needed. Doctors know that patients' treatment regimens often need to be recalibrated over time—change works the same way.

Of course, sometimes you'll set your sights on change and, despite adjusting your approach and trying every trick in the book (literally in *this* book), you'll find that you still aren't where you want to be. Let's say you were hoping to kick-start a gym habit, but you just can't get it off the ground. When you keep hitting a wall on a particular goal, it's time to step back, reassess, and think about the bigger picture instead of making yourself miserable.

Most goals are just a means to a greater end. Hitting the gym is just *one* way of getting in shape. If improving your fitness is your broader aim, there are other ways to achieve it. You could use a walking desk at work, join a basketball team, add a brisk stroll to your lunch break, change your commute, or exercise at home with an app. Maybe working out at the gym isn't the best path to fitness for you, but another path could put success within reach.

If you've tried really hard to achieve a goal using all of the wizardry that you can muster but still aren't seeing results, it's a good time to consider new ways to reach the same end and give yourself a fresh start. Not only do the obstacles that you face require tailored solutions; you need *tailored goals* that acknowledge and match your strengths and weaknesses. Pain points are different for every person—a goal that feels like a chore for one person can be a pleasure for someone else, and we know from Mary Poppins that finding a path that you enjoy can work wonders.

With a tailored approach that suits you and your circumstances, change is within your grasp. My hope is that this book can be your guide every step of the way. By diagnosing the internal obstacles you face and *consistently* using solutions customized to help you succeed, evidence and experience show that you really can get from where you are to where you want to be.

Acknowledgments

When I started this project, I hadn't the foggiest idea what it would take to write a book for a popular audience. I'm so grateful for the support I received from an extraordinary group of people who were patient, forgiving, and generous with their time as well as their advice.

First and most important, thank you to my amazing husband, Cullen Blake, who not only read every chapter repeatedly and let me run book ideas by him at all hours but who also took on far more than his fair share of pandemic parenting and housework so I could finish this beast. This book would not exist were it not for your unending support and generosity, Cullen, not to mention the inspiration you provide every day (you're the best problem solver I know).

Thank you also to my parents, Ray and Bev Milkman, for their constant love, for being my biggest champions, and for moving to Philadelphia to help with childcare and much, much more. I'm so grateful to you. And I'll admit now that getting me into competitive tennis all those years ago might not have been so crazy—I learned a thing or two about life along the way.

To Cormac Blake, my loving and energetic son, thank you for your excitement about this book. When I was midway through writing, your preschool teachers told me that you had started a new fad—you'd talked your three- and four-year-old classmates into writing books, just like your mom; my heart nearly burst with pride. While I opted not to use your suggested title for this manuscript (since *The Great Delaware* seemed a bit off topic), these pages were still shaped by you in more ways than you know.

My book agent, Rafe Sagalyn, served as an exceptional guide on this adventure. Rafe, I'm so grateful for your insights, wisdom, and patience with my neuroses. Thank you in particular for helping me find my way to Niki Papadopoulos and the whole team at Portfolio (including Adrian Zackheim, Kimberly Meilun, Regina Andreoni, Amanda Lang, Tara Gilbride, Stefanie Brody, Jarrod Taylor, and Brian Lemus)—I could not have asked for a more extraordinary editor or publishing group. Niki, thank you for patiently coaching me on how to craft a chapter with a narrative arc and teaching me where to pause and dig deeper. The guidance and support you provided were invaluable.

Angela Duckworth not only read every word of this book and made invaluable improvements but also launched me on the most exciting adventure of my academic career, which led me to write it. Many of the ideas in these pages were formed in conversation with you, Angela. Thank you for your partnership and inspiration on this intellectual journey and for your constant support.

As a first-time writer, it truly took a village to get me to the finish line. I'm particularly grateful to Kassie Brabaw, who spent nearly two years as my book assistant, helping improve everything in this tome from the prose to the bibliography. Kassie, I was so lucky to find you and am so thankful for all the time and energy you put into making this book as good as it could be. Thank you also to Gareth Cook, Kate Rodemann, Jamie Ryerson, Katie Shonk, Mike Hernan, and Andy Cassel for reading and offering constructive editorial comments on parts (and in some cases all) of this book, and to my student research assistants Meghan Chung, Karen Herrera, Michelle Huang, and Ilyssa Reyes for combing through the final manuscript in search of typos.

I'm also incredibly grateful to the many generous friends, family, and colleagues who took the time to read a first draft of this manuscript and provide invaluable feedback. I've thanked some of you already (Cullen, Angela, Mom and Dad), but thank you also to Modupe Akinola, Max Bazerman, Rachel Bernard, Dolly Chugh, Annie Duke, Linnea Gandhi, Guy Kawasaki, Sendhil Mullainathan, and Aria Woodley for your invaluable input. I'm also grateful to my friend Nathaniel Pincus-Roth for all of his input on titles, subtitles, and cover designs.

None of my ongoing work on behavior change would be possible without the incredible research staff, past and present, at the Behavior Change for Good Initiative. Thank you so much to Dena Gromet, Joseph Kay, Tim Lee, Yeji Park, Heather Graci, Aneesh Rai, Lauri Bonacorsi, Hung Ho, and Pepi Pandiloski. I'm also incredibly grateful to the amazing research assistants who helped with this book, including Graelin Mandel, Canyon Kornicker, and Yunzi Lu.

Thank you to everyone involved with the *Choiceology* podcast I host for your patience with me when I begged to move recording sessions around to accommodate book deadlines; for finding dozens of amazing stories about behavior change for *Choiceology*, many of which eventually made their way into the pages of this book; and for all you taught me about how to communicate about science. A particularly big shout-out is owed to showrunner Andy Sheppard from Pacific Content, but thanks also to Pacific Content's Annie Rueter and to Charles Schwab's Patrick Ricci, Matt Bucher, Mark Riepe, and Tami Dorsey. I'm so lucky to work with all of you!

I would be remiss if I didn't also thank my many extraordinary academic collaborators on the work that led me to write this book. In particular, I'm so grateful to Max Bazerman (who is truly the world's greatest adviser), John Beshears (who taught me how to be a good scientist and collaborator and how to think like an economist), Todd Rogers (who got me hooked on "nudging" and libertarian paternalism and introduced me to Angela), Hengchen Dai (my first student and a ray of sunshine who gave my career a fresh start), and Dolly Chugh and Modupe Akinola (my "sisters" and fellow No Clubbers—how would I survive without your support?). Thank you also to my amazing students Edward Chang, Aneesh Rai, and Erika Kirgios, who were heroically patient with me when I was writing this book and who inspire me every day with their energy and commitment to making the world a better place through science. And thank you to my other brilliant collaborators whose work appears in these pages, including: Shlomo Benartzi, Colin Camerer, Gretchen Chapman, James Choi, Bob Cialdini, Cindy Cryder, Lauren Eskreis-Winkler, Amanda Geiser, Rachel Gershon, James Gross, Samantha Horn, Alexa Hubbard, Steven Jones, Tim Kautz, Joowon Klusowski, Ariella Kristal, Rahul Ladhania, David Laibson, Sunny Lee, George Loewenstein, Jens Ludwig, Brigitte Madrian, David Mao, Katie Mehr, Barbara Mellers, Julia Minson, Rob Mislavsky, Sendhil Mullainathan, Pepi Pandiloski, Jason Riis, Silvia Saccardo, Marissa Sharif, Jann Spiess, Gaurav Suri, Joachim

Talloen, Jamie Taxer, Yaacov Trope, Lyle Ungar, Kevin Volpp, Ashley Whillans, and Jonathan Zinman.

To the many other extraordinary scientists whose research is featured in this manuscript and who checked to ensure I hadn't said anything inaccurate, thank you for your inspiring work and your time. That list includes Dan Ariely, John Austin, Linda Babcock, Scott Carrell, Gary Charness, Alia Crum, Ayelet Fishbach, Jana Gallus, Alan Gerber, Uri Gneezy, Noah Goldstein, Peter Gollwitzer, Kirabo Jackson, Dean Karlan, Julia Minson, Ethan Mollick, Mitesh Patel, Marissa Sharif, Stephen Spiller, Kevin Werbach, Wendy Wood, David Yeager, and Erez Yoeli.

I'm also very grateful to the students, friends, and leaders who let me tell their stories in this book, including Judy Chevalier, Jordan Goldberg, Karen Herrera, Steve Honeywell, Bob Pass, Prashant Srivastava, Prasad Setty, and Nick Winter.

Finally, a big thank you to my speaking agent, David Lavin, who encouraged me to write this book and helped nudge it toward a happy home at Portfolio.

Notes

INTRODUCTION

1 **When he turned pro:** Andre Agassi, *Open: An Autobiography* (New York: Vintage Books, 2009), 101.

1 **But by 1994:** McCarton Ackerman, "Andre Agassi: From Rebel to Philosopher," ATP Tour, July 9, 2020, accessed August 31, 2020, www.atptour.com/en/news/atp-heritage-agassi-no-1-fedex-atp-rankings.

1 **splashy ad campaign:** Steve Tignor, "1989: Image Is Everything—Andre Agassi's Infamous Ad," Tennis.com, August 30, 2015, accessed October 1, 2020, www.tennis.com/pro-game/2015/08/image-everything-andre-agassis-infamous-ad/55425.

1 **first-round flameout:** Agassi, *Open*, 172.

1 **third-round defeat:** Agassi, *Open*, 117.

1 **ranking kept slipping:** Andre Agassi Rankings History, ATP Tour, accessed August 31, 2020, www.atptour.com/en/players/andre-agassi/a092/rankings-history.

2 **coach of ten years:** "TENNIS; Agassi Has Streisand, but Loses Bollettieri," *New York Times*, July 10, 1993, accessed August 31, 2020, www.nytimes.com/1993/07/10/sports/tennis-agassi-has-streisand-but-loses-bollettieri.html.

2 **Agassi learned the news:** Agassi, *Open*, 179.

2 found himself eating dinner: Agassi, *Open*, 185.

2 Gilbert, then thirty-two: Brad Gilbert Rankings History, ATP Tour, accessed August 31, 2020, www.atptour.com/en/players/brad-gilbert /g016/rankings-history.

2 reaching number four: Gilbert Rankings History, ATP Tour.

2 Gilbert had detailed: Brad Gilbert, *Winning Ugly* (New York: Fireside, 1993).

2 After reading the book: Agassi, *Open*, 185.

2 Agassi's manager opened: Agassi, 186.

3 he'd learned to go: Jen Vafidis, "Andre Agassi: Remembering Tennis Legend's Golden Olympic Moment," *Rolling Stone*, July 27, 2016, accessed August 31, 2020, www.rollingstone.com/culture/culture-sports /andre-agassi-remembering-tennis-legends-golden-olympic-moment -248765.

3 "Hit *harder!*" he'd yell: Agassi, *Open*, 28.

3 "Stop thinking about yourself": Agassi, *Open*, 187.

3 Gilbert's uncanny ability: "Winning Ugly: Mental Warfare in Tennis— Tales from Tour and Lessons from the Master," *Publishers Weekly*, June 1993, accessed October 1, 2020, www.publishersweekly.com/978 -1-55972-169-1.

3 "Instead of you succeeding": Agassi, *Open*, 187.

4 "That's our guy": Agassi, 188.

4 A few months later: Robin Finn, "U.S. Open '94; The New Agassi Style Now Has Substance," *New York Times*, September 12, 1994, accessed August 31, 2020, www.nytimes.com/1994/09/12/sports/us -open-94-the-new-agassi-style-now-has-substance.html.

4 There was 550,000 dollars: "U.S. Open Prize Money Progression," ESPN, July 11, 2012, accessed August 31, 2020, www.espn.com/espn /wire/_/section/tennis/id/8157332.

4 His opponent was Michael Stich: Finn, "U.S. Open '94."

4 the set was tied: Agassi, *Open*, 196.

5 "Go for his forehand": Agassi, 196.

5 first unseeded player: Finn, "U.S. Open '94."

8 the "nudge movement": Richard H. Thaler and Cass R. Sunstein, "Libertarian Paternalism," *American Economic Review* 93, no. 2 (2003): 175–79, DOI:10.1257/000282803321947001.

8 an estimated 40 percent: Steven A. Schroeder, "We Can Do Better—Improving the Health of the American People," *New England Journal of Medicine* 357, no. 12 (2007): 1221–28, DOI:10.1056/NEJMsa 073350.

10 collaborate with dozens: Behavior Change for Good Initiative, "Creating Enduring Behavior Change," Wharton School, University of Pennsylvania, accessed February 3, 2020. https://bcfg.wharton.upenn.edu.

10 Our collective research: David S. Yeager, Paul Hanselman, Gregory M. Walton, Jared S. Murray, Robert Crosnoe, Chandra Muller, Elizabeth Tipton et al., "A National Experiment Reveals Where a Growth Mindset Improves Achievement," *Nature* 573, no. 7774 (2019): 364–69, DOI:10.1038/s41586-019-1466-y.

10 medical practices cut down: Daniella Meeker, Tara K. Knight, Mark W. Friedberg, Jeffrey A. Linder, Noah J. Goldstein, Craig R. Fox, Alan Rothfeld, Guillermo Diaz, and Jason N. Doctor, "Nudging Guideline-Concordant Antibiotic Prescribing: A Randomized Clinical Trial," *JAMA Internal Medicine* 174, no. 3 (2014): 425–31, DOI: 10.1001/jamainternmed.2013.14191.

10 nonprofits increase volunteering: Aneesh Rai, Marissa Sharif, Edward Chang, Katherine L. Milkman, and Angela Duckworth, "The Benefits of Specificity and Flexibility on Goal-Directed Behavior over Time" (working paper, 2020).

10 employers boost enrollment: John Beshears, Hengchen Dai, Katherine L. Milkman, and Shlomo Benartzi, "Using Fresh Starts to Nudge Increased Retirement Savings" (working paper, 2020).

10 kick-start an exercise habit: John Beshears, Hae Nim Lee, Katherine L. Milkman, Robert Mislavsky, and Jessica Wisdom, "Creating Exercise Habits: The Trade-Off between Flexibility and Routinization," *Management Science* (October 2020), https://doi.org/10.1287/mnsc .2020.3706.

10 improve their diet: Eric M. VanEpps, Julie S. Downs, and George Loewenstein, "Advance Ordering for Healthier Eating? Field Experiments on the Relationship between the Meal Order–Consumption Time Delay and Meal Content," *Journal of Marketing Research* 53, no. 3 (2016): 369–80, DOI:10.1509/jmr.14.0234.

10 **increase the balance:** Hal E. Hershfield, Stephen Shu, and Shlomo Benartzi, "Temporal Reframing and Participation in a Savings Program: A Field Experiment," *Marketing Science* 39, no. 6 (2020): 1033–1201, https://doi.org/10.1287/mksc.2019.1177.

10 **get to the polls on:** David W. Nickerson and Todd Rogers. "Do You Have a Voting Plan?: Implementation Intentions, Voter Turnout, and Organic Plan Making," *Psychological Science* 21, no. 2 (2010): 194–99, DOI:10.1177/0956797609359326.

11 **Agassi's surprise victory:** Agassi Rankings History, ATP Tour.

11 **a title he would:** John Berkok, "On This Day: Andre Agassi Takes over Top Spot for the First Time in 1995," Tennis.com, April 10, 2020, accessed September 30, 2020, www.tennis.com/pro-game/2020/04 /on-this-day-andre-agassi-reaches-world-no-1-first-time-1995-25th -anniversary/88332.

CHAPTER 1: GETTING STARTED

13 **Google had raked in:** Google Inc., Form 10-K for the fiscal year ended December 31, 2011 (filed January 26, 2012), 25, accessed March 31, 2020, www.sec.gov/Archives/edgar/data/1288776/000119312512025 336/d260164d10k.htm#toc260164_8.

14 **improving their productivity:** Shai Bernstein, Timothy McQuade, and Richard Townsend, "Do Household Wealth Shocks Affect Productivity? Evidence from Innovative Workers During the Great Recession," National Bureau of Economic Research, working paper w24011 (November 2017), DOI:10.3386/w24011.

14 **health and financial security:** Timothy Gubler, Ian Larkin, and Lamar Pierce, "Doing Well by Making Well: The Impact of Corporate Wellness Programs on Employee Productivity," *Management Science* 64, no. 11 (November 2018): 4967–87, DOI:10.1287/mnsc.2017.2883.

14 **Prasad Setty, a Wharton alum:** Prasad Setty, conversation with the author at Google PiLab Research Summit, Mountain View, California, May 11, 2012.

14 **offered its employees:** Rebecca J. Mitchell and Paul Bates, "Measuring Health-Related Productivity Loss," *Population Health Management* 14, no. 2 (April 2011): 93–98, DOI:10.1089/pop.2010.0014.

14 **some ideal moment:** Prasad Setty, conversation.

15 **tens of thousands of babies:** GBD 2013 Mortality and Causes of Death Collaborators, "Global, Regional, and National Age–Sex Specific All-Cause and Cause-Specific Mortality for 240 Causes of Death, 1990–2013: A Systematic Analysis for the Global Burden of Disease Study 2013," *The Lancet* 385, no. 9963 (January 2015): 117–71, DOI:10.1016/s0140-6736(14)61682-2.

15 **SIDS has been:** "Infant Mortality," Centers for Disease Control and Prevention, last reviewed March 27, 2019, accessed July 9, 2020, www .cdc.gov/reproductivehealth/maternalinfanthealth/infantmortality .htm.

16 **discovered that infants:** Marian Willinger, Howard J. Hoffman, and Robert B. Hartford, "Infant Sleep Position and Risk for Sudden Infant Death Syndrome: Report of Meeting Held January 13 and 14, 1994, National Institutes of Health, Bethesda, MD," *Pediatrics* 93, no. 5 (1994): 814–819.

16 **U.S. government launched:** Felicia L. Trachtenberg, Elisabeth A. Haas, Hannah C. Kinney, Christina Stanley, and Henry F. Krous, "Risk Factor Changes for Sudden Infant Death Syndrome after Initiation of Back-to-Sleep Campaign," *Pediatrics* 129, no. 4 (March 2012): 630–38, DOI:10.1542/peds.2011-1419.

16 **telling people how many calories:** Bryan Bollinger, Phillip Leslie, and Alan Sorensen, "Calorie Posting in Chain Restaurants," *American Economic Journal: Economic Policy* 3, no. 1 (February 2011): 91–128, DOI:10.1257/pol.3.1.91.

16 **to persuade Americans:** Centers for Disease Control and Prevention, "CDC's Advisory Committee on Immunization Practices (ACIP) Recommends Universal Annual Influenza Vaccination," accessed May 17, 2019, www.cdc.gov/media/pressrel/2010/r100224.htm.

16 **43 percent of Americans:** Centers for Disease Control and Prevention, "Flu Vaccination Coverage, United States, 2016–17 Influenza Season," accessed May 17, 2019, www.cdc.gov/flu/fluvaxview/cover age-1617estimates.htm.

16 **up from 39 percent:** Katherine M. Harris, Jürgen Maurer, Lori Uscher-Pines, Arthur L. Kellermann, and Nicole Lurie, "Seasonal Flu Vaccination: Why Don't More Americans Get It?" RAND Corporation, 2011, accessed May 17, 2019, www.rand.org/pubs/research_briefs /RB9572.html.

16 **Between 1993 and 2010:** American Academy of Pediatrics, "Reducing Sudden Infant Death with 'Back to Sleep,'" accessed May 17, 2019,

www.aap.org/en-us/advocacy-and-policy/aap-health-initiatives
/7-great-achievements/Pages/Reducing-Sudden-Infant-Death-with
-Back-to-.aspx.

19 **Take Scott Harrison:** Scott Harrison, *Thirst* (New York: Crown Publishing, 2018), 49–53.

19 **rather than perceiving:** Michael S. Shum, "The Role of Temporal Landmarks in Autobiographical Memory Processes," *Psychological Bulletin* 124, no. 3 (November 1998): 423–42, DOI:10.1037/0033-29 09.124.3.423.

20 **When we're labeled:** Christopher J. Bryan, Gregory M. Walton, Todd Rogers, and Carol S. Dweck, "Motivating Voter Turnout by Invoking the Self," *PNAS* 108, no. 31 (August 2011): 12653–56, DOI:10.1073 /pnas.1103343108.

20 **"carrot eaters" (instead of people:** Susan A. Gelman and Gail D. Heyman, "Carrot-Eaters and Creature-Believers: The Effects of Lexicalization on Children's Inferences about Social Categories," *Psychological Science* 10, no. 6 (1999): 489–93, DOI:10.1111/1467-9280.00194.

20 **"Shakespeare readers" (instead of people:** Gregory M. Walton and Mahzarin R. Banaji, "Being What You Say: The Effect of Essentialist Linguistic Labels on Preferences," *Social Cognition* 22, no. 2 (2004): 193–213, DOI:10.1521/soco.22.2.193.35463.

20 **Ray used the arrival:** Katy Milkman, "A Clean Slate," *Choiceology*, January 7, 2019, accessed December 20, 2019, www.schwab.com /resource-center/insights/content/choiceology-season-2-episode-5.

21 **every January 1:** John C. Norcross, Marci S. Mrykalo, and Matthew D. Blagys, "'Auld lang Syne': Success Predictors, Change Processes, and Self-Reported Outcomes of New Year's Resolvers and Nonresolvers," *Journal of Clinical Psychology* 58, no. 4 (April 2002): 397–405, DOI:10.1002/jclp.1151.

22 **we gathered information:** Hengchen Dai, Katherine L. Milkman, and Jason Riis, "The Fresh Start Effect: Temporal Landmarks Motivate Aspirational Behavior," *Management Science* 60, no. 10 (June 2014): 1–20, DOI:10.1287/mnsc.2014.1901.

22 **People feel distanced:** Hengchen Dai, Katherine L. Milkman, and Jason Riis, "Put Your Imperfections behind You: Temporal Landmarks Spur Goal Initiation When They Signal New Beginnings," *Psychological Science* 26, no. 12 (November 2015): 1927–36, DOI: 10.1177/0956797615605818.

23 **These new beginnings:** Wendy Liu, "Focusing on Desirability: The Effect of Decision Interruption and Suspension on Preferences," *Journal of Consumer Research* 35, no. 4 (December 2008): 640–52, DOI: 10.1086/592126.

23 **Looking at the caged gorillas:** Bob Pass, telephone conversation with the author, January 31, 2020.

24 **two psychologists surveyed:** Todd F. Heatherton and Patricia A. Nichols, "Personal Accounts of Successful Versus Failed Attempts at Life Change," *Personality and Social Psychology Bulletin* 20, no. 6 (December 1994): 664–75, DOI:10.1177/0146167294206005.

25 **the London Underground strike:** Shaun Larcom, Ferdinand Rauch, and Tim Willems, "The Benefits of Forced Experimentation: Striking Evidence from the London Underground Network," *Quarterly Journal of Economics* 132, no. 4 (November 2017): 2019–55, DOI:10.1093/qje/qjx020.

25 **a study of Texas:** Wendy Wood, Leona Tam, and Melissa Guerrero-Witt, "Changing Circumstances, Disrupting Habits," *Journal of Personality and Social Psychology* 88, no. 6 (June 2005): 918–33, DOI: 10.1037/0022-3514.88.6.918.

26 **Hengchen, Jason, and I had seen:** Dai et al., "The Fresh Start Effect," 1–20.

27 **When Hengchen analyzed:** Hengchen Dai, "A Double-Edged Sword: How and Why Resetting Performance Metrics Affects Motivation," *Organizational Behavior and Human Decision Processes* 148 (September 2018): 12–29, DOI:10.1016/j.obhdp.2018.06.002.

28 **shortstop Orlando Cabrera:** Orlando Cabrera stats, ESPN, accessed June 8, 2020, www.espn.com/mlb/player/stats/_/id/3739/orlando-cabrera.

28 **Jarrod Saltalamacchia learned:** Jarrod Saltalamacchia stats, ESPN, accessed February 8, 2020, www.espn.com/mlb/player/stats/_/id/28663/jarrod-saltalamacchia.

29 **In experiments where she hired:** Hengchen Dai, "A Double-Edged Sword," 12–29.

29 **holiday breaks turned out:** Daniel Acland and Matthew R. Levy, "Naivete, Projection Bias, and Habit Formation in Gym Attendance," *Management Science* 61, no. 1 (January 2015): 146–160, DOI:10.1287/mnsc.2014.2091.

29 **failed to resume:** Katherine L. Milkman, Julia A. Minson, and Kevin G. M. Volpp, "Holding the Hunger Games Hostage at the Gym: An Evaluation of Temptation Bundling," *Management Science* 60, no. 2 (November 2013): 283–99, DOI:10.1287/mnsc.2013.1784.

30 **Past research has shown:** Richard H. Thaler and Shlomo Benartzi, "Save More Tomorrow™: Using Behavioral Economics to Increase Employee Saving," *Journal of Political Economy* 112, no. S1 (2004): S164–S187, DOI:10.1086/380085.

30 **Hengchen and I teamed up:** John Beshears, Katherine Milkman, Hengchen Dai, and Shlomo Benartzi, "Using Fresh Starts to Nudge Increased Retirement Savings" (working paper, 2020).

31 **In one study, we described March 20:** Dai et al., "Put Your Imperfections behind You," 1927–36.

31 **In another study, we described May 14:** Dai et al., "Put Your Imperfections behind You."

32 **Follow-up research by:** Marie Hennecke and Benjamin Converse, "Next Week, Next Month, Next Year: How Perceived Temporal Boundaries Affect Initiation Expectations," *Social Psychological and Personality Science* 8, no. 8 (March 2017): 918–26, DOI:10.1177/1948550617691099.

32 **When calendars depicted:** Mariya Davydenko and Johanna Peetz, "Does It Matter If a Week Starts on Monday or Sunday? How Calendar Format Can Boost Goal Motivation," *Journal of Experimental Social Psychology* 82 (2019): 231–37, DOI:10.1016/j.jesp.2019.02.005.

32 **Retirement planning matters:** Kathleen Craig and Forbes Finance Council, "The State of Savings in America," *Forbes*, February 10, 2020, accessed October 2, 2020, www.forbes.com/sites/forbesfinance council/2020/02/10/the-state-of-savings-in-america/#48a61 d5d48fb.

33 **labeled fresh start:** Beshears et al., "Using Fresh Starts."

33 **Google programmers built:** Prasad Setty, email with the author, July 1, 2019.

34 **From nonprofits timing:** Laszlo Bock, conversation with the author at Humu webinar, July 15, 2020.

34 **One third of Americans':** Tara Parker-Pope, "Will Your Resolutions Last Until February?" *Well* (blog), *New York Times*, December 31, 2007, accessed September 28, 2020, http://well.blogs.nytimes.com /2007/12/31/will-your-resolutions-last-to-february.

34 **"If you're not in the game":** Eric Spitznagel, "David Hasselhoff: The Interview," *Men's Health*, May 17, 2012, accessed June 25, 2020, www.menshealth.com/trending-news/a19555092/david-hasselhoff -interview.

CHAPTER 2: IMPULSIVITY

37 **a hundred thousand passengers:** Stockholm Regional Council, "AB Storstockholms Lokaltrafik SL och Länet 2018," accessed October 6, 2020, www.sll.se/globalassets/2.-kollektivtrafik/fakta-om-sl-och-lanet /sl_och_lanet_2018.pdf.

38 **Video taken of the exit:** Rolighetsteorin, "Piano Stairs—TheFun Theory.com," YouTube video, 1:47, October 7, 2009, www.youtube .com/watch?time_continue=6&v=2lXh2n0aPyw.

38 **the film reports:** Rolighetsteorin, "Piano Stairs."

38 **Knowing that walking:** Dena M. Bravata, Crystal Smith-Spangler, Vandana Sundaram, Allison L. Gienger, Nancy Lin, Robyn Lewis, Christopher D. Stave, Ingram Olkin, and John R. Sirard, "Using Pedometers to Increase Physical Activity and Improve Health: A Systematic Review," *Journal of the American Medical Association* 298, no. 19 (2007): 2296–2304.

39 **Economists call this tendency:** Ted O'Donoghue and Matthew Rabin, "Present Bias: Lessons Learned and to Be Learned," *American Economic Review* 105, no. 5 (2015): 273–79, DOI:10.1257/aer.p20151085.

40 **Disney classic *Mary Poppins*:** *Mary Poppins*, directed by Robert Stevenson (1964; Burbank, CA: Buena Vista Distribution Company, 1980), VHS.

40 **Disney tasked the renowned:** Jasper Rees, "A Spoonful of Sugar: Robert Sherman, 1925–2012, The Arts Desk," last modified March 6, 2012, accessed July 23, 2019, www.theartsdesk.com/film/spoonful -sugar-robert-sherman-1925-2012.

41 **two thirds of respondents:** Kaitlin Woolley and Ayelet Fishbach, "For the Fun of It: Harnessing Immediate Rewards to Increase Persistence in Long-Term Goals," *Journal of Consumer Research* 42, no. 6 (2016): 952–66, DOI:10.1093/jcr/ucv098.

41 **This is why:** Stefano DellaVigna and Ulrike Malmendier, "Paying Not to Go to the Gym," *American Economic Review* 96, no. 3 (2006): 694–719, DOI:10.1257/aer.96.3.694.

41 **register for online classes:** Justin Reich and José Ruipérez-Valiente, "The MOOC Pivot," *Science* 363, no. 6423 (2019): 130–31, DOI:10 .1126/science.aav7958.

41 **purchase family-size chips:** Klaus Wertenbroch, "Consumption Self-Control by Rationing Purchase Quantities of Virtue and Vice," *Marketing Science* 17, no. 4 (1998): 317–37, DOI:10.1287/mksc.17.4.317.

42 **Ayelet and Kaitlin encouraged:** Woolley and Fishbach, "For the Fun of It," 952–66.

42 **encouraged more exercise:** Woolley and Fishbach, "For the Fun of It," 952–66.

43 **Although adults have:** Cinzia R. De Luca, Stephen J. Wood, Vicki Anderson, Jo-Anne Buchanan, Tina M. Proffitt, Kate Mahony, and Christos Pantelis, "Normative Data from the Cantab. I: Development of Executive Function over the Lifespan," *Journal of Clinical and Experimental Neuropsychology* 25, no. 2 (2010): 242–54, DOI:10.1076 /jcen.25.2.242.13639.

46 **As we'd expected:** Katherine L. Milkman, Julia A. Minson, and Kevin G. M. Volpp, "Holding the Hunger Games Hostage at the Gym: An Evaluation of Temptation Bundling," *Management Science* 60, no. 2 (November 2013): 283–99, DOI:10.1287/mnsc.2013.1784.

47 **partnership with Audible:** Erika L. Kirgios, Graelin H. Mandel, Yeji Park, Katherine L. Milkman, Dena Gromet, Joseph Kay, and Angela L. Duckworth, "Teaching Temptation Bundling to Boost Exercise: A Field Experiment," *Organizational Behavior and Human Decision Processes* (working paper, 2020).

48 **Much to the surprise of many:** Woolley and Fishbach, "For the Fun of It," 952–66.

50 **volunteer labor force:** Jana Gallus, telephone conversation with the author, May 17, 2019.

52 **volunteers who received recognition:** Jana Gallus, "Fostering Public Good Contributions with Symbolic Awards: A Large-Scale Natural Field Experiment at Wikipedia," *Management Science* 63, no. 12, (2017): 3999–4015, DOI:10.1287/mnsc.2016.2540.

52 **something called "gamification":** Kevin Werbach, conversation with the author, Philadelphia, June 25, 2019.

52 **Cisco, a technology conglomerate:** Katie Gibbs Masters, "5 Tips to Becoming a 'Savvy' Social Media Marketer," Cisco Blogs, April 22, 2013,

accessed March 30, 2020, https://blogs.cisco.com/socialmedia/5-tips-to -becoming-a-savvy-social-media-marketer.

52 **Microsoft created leaderboards:** Oliver Chiang, "When Playing Videogames at Work Makes Dollars and Sense," *Forbes*, August 9, 2010, www.forbes.com/2010/08/09/microsoft-workplace-training -technology-videogames.html#2f408a176b85.

52 **SAP created a game:** "Examples of Gamification in the Workplace," *Racoon Gang*, April 19, 2018, https://raccoongang.com/blog/examples-gamification-workplace.

53 **Ethan and Nancy worked:** Ethan R. Mollick and Nancy Rothbard, "Mandatory Fun: Consent, Gamification and the Impact of Games at Work," Wharton School Research Paper Series, SSRN (September 30, 2014), https://papers.ssrn.com/sol3/papers.cfm?abstract_id =2277103.

53 **surprised to find:** Ethan Mollick, conversation with the author, Philadelphia, June 20, 2019.

54 **questions were designed:** Johan Huizinga, *Homo Ludens: A Study of the Play-Element in Culture* (New York: Roy Publishers, 1950), 10.

54 **"entered the magic circle," a term:** Katie Selen and Eric Zimmerman, *Rules of Play: Game Design Fundamentals* (Cambridge, MA: MIT Press, 2003), 94.

55 **Consider the experience:** Katy Milkman, "A Spoonful of Sugar," *Choiceology*, May 25, 2020, accessed October 5, 2020, www.schwab .com/resource-center/insights/content/choiceology-season-5-episode-6.

56 **twelve-week experiment:** Mitesh Patel et al., "Effect of a Game-Based Intervention Designed to Enhance Social Incentives to Increase Physical Activity Among Families," *JAMA Internal Medicine* 177, no. 11 (2017): 1586–93, DOI:10.1001/jamainternmed.2017.3458.

57 **a tech company:** Taylor Lorenz, "How Asana Built the Best Company Culture in Tech," *Fast Company*, last modified March 29, 2017, accessed July 23, 2019, www.fastcompany.com/3069240/how-asana -built-the-best-company-culture-in-tech.

57 **The Farmer's Dog:** "These are the 18 Coolest Companies to Work for in NYC," Uncubed, accessed July 23, 2019, https://uncubed.com /daily/these-are-the-coolest-companies-to-work-for-in-nyc.

58 **Virtual happy hours became:** Roy Maurer, "Virtual Happy Hours Help Co-Workers, Industry Peers Stay Connected," Society for Human

Resource Management, April 6, 2020, accessed June 24, 2020, www
.shrm.org/hr-today/news/hr-news/pages/virtual-happy-hours-help
-coworkers-stay-connected.aspx.

CHAPTER 3: PROCRASTINATION

61 **Omar Andaya was:** Nava Ashraf, Dean S. Karlan, Wesley Yin, and
Marc Shotland, "Evaluating Microsavings Programs: Green Bank of
the Philippines (A)," Harvard Business School Case no. 909-062 (June
2009, revised February 2014), www.hbs.edu/faculty/Pages/item.aspx
?num=37449.

61 **no money saved:** Pew Trusts, "What Resources Do Families Have
for Financial Emergencies?" Pew Trusts, November 18, 2015, accessed July 26, 2019, www.pewtrusts.org/en/research-and-analysis
/issue-briefs/2015/11/emergency-savings-what-resources-do-families
-have-for-financial-emergencies.

61 **41 percent of families:** Pew Trusts, "What Resources Do Families
Have?"

62 **below the poverty line:** National Statistical Coordination Board, Population Income and Employment Division and Health Education and
Social Welfare Division, *Philippine Poverty Statistics* (Makati City,
Philippines: 2000), https://psa.gov.ph/sites/default/files/1997%20Phil
ippine%20Poverty%20Statistics.pdf.

62 **he was excited:** Dean Karlan, email with the author, May 7, 2020.

62 **should give his customers:** Ashraf et al., "Evaluating Microsavings
Programs."

63 **"temptation take them":** Dan Ariely, *Predictably Irrational: The Hid-
den Forces That Shape Our Decisions* (New York: HarperCollins
Publishers, 2008), 141.

64 **Dan and Klaus began:** Dan Ariely and Klaus Wertenbroch, "Procrastination, Deadlines, and Performance: Self-Control by Precommitment," *Psychological Science* 13, no. 3 (2002): 219–24, DOI:10.1111
/1467-9280.00441.

65 **In the Philippines, Nava:** Nava Ashraf, Dean Karlan, and Wesley Yin,
"Tying Odysseus to the Mast: Evidence from a Commitment Savings
Product in the Philippines," *Quarterly Journal of Economics* 121, no.
2 (2006): 635–72, DOI:10.1162/qjec.2006.121.2.635.

66 Perhaps most famously, in: Homer, *The Odyssey*, trans. Robert Fitzgerald (New York: Vintage Books, 1990), 215–16.

67 he locked up all: Adèle Hugo and Charles E. Wilbour, *Victor Hugo, by a Witness of His Life* (New York: Carleton, 1864), 156.

67 In 1955, an economist: Robert Henry Strotz, "Myopia and Inconsistency in Dynamic Utility Maximization," *Review of Economic Studies* 23, no. 3 (1955): 165–80, DOI:10.1007/978-1-349-15492-0_10.

67 exploring these strategies: Richard H. Thaler and Hersh M. Shefrin, "An Economic Theory of Self-Control," *Journal of Political Economy* 89, no. 2 (1981): 392–406, DOI:10.1086/260971.

67 a name to them: "commitment devices": Thomas Schelling, *Strategies of Commitment and Other Essays* (Cambridge, MA: Harvard University Press, 2006).

68 Whenever you do something: Todd Rogers, Katherine L. Milkman, and Kevin G. Volpp, "Commitment Devices: Using Initiatives to Change Behavior," *Journal of the American Medical Association* 311, no. 20 (2014): 2065–66, DOI:10.1001/jama.2014.3485.

68 an app like Moment: Moment app, "Moment: Less Phone, More Real Life," Apple, https://inthemoment.io.

68 putting your name on: Ryan Ocello, "Self-Exclusion List Violations Remain a Small but Persistent Problem for PA Land-Based Casinos," Penn Bets, February 14, 2018, accessed July 26, 2019, www.pennbets.com/mohegan-sun-pa-self-exclusion-violations.

68 economists who pitched: Ashraf, Karlan, and Yin, "Tying Odysseus to the Mast," 635–72.

69 When the results: Dean Karlan, email conversation with the author, February 15, 2020.

69 Dan and Klaus conducted: Dan Ariely and Klaus Wertenbroch, "Procrastination, Deadlines, and Performance: Self-Control by Precommitment," *Psychological Science* 13, no. 3 (2002): 219–24, DOI:10.1111/1467-9280.00441.

70 not likely to be: Katherine L. Milkman, Julia A. Minson, and Kevin G. M. Volpp, "Holding the Hunger Games Hostage at the Gym: An Evaluation of Temptation Bundling," *Management Science* 60, no. 2 (November 2013): 283–99, DOI:10.1287/mnsc.2013.1784.

71 This is the question: Jordan Goldberg, lecture at Wharton School at University of Pennsylvania, February 21, 2019.

71 cofounder of stickK: "Biography: Jordan Goldberg," Expert Word/ Author Index, stickK, accessed October 7, 2020, www.stickk.com /blogs/author?authorId=31&category=expertWord.

72 Not long ago, I spoke: Nick Winter, telephone conversation with the author, July 15, 2019.

72 Back in 2012: Nick Winter, "The Motivation Hacker," nickwinter .net, April 6, 2013, accessed December 12, 2019, www.nickwinter .net/the-motivation-hacker.

73 adventuring: *The Motivation Hacker*: Nick Winter, *The Motivation Hacker* (self-published, 2013).

74 two thousand smokers: Xavier Giné, Dean Karlan, and Jonathan Zinman, "Put Your Money Where Your Butt Is: A Commitment Contract for Smoking Cessation," *American Economic Journal: Applied Economics* 2, no. 4 (2010): 213–35, DOI:10.1257/app.2.4.213.

74 Similar cash commitment: Heather Royer, Mark Stehr, and Justin Sydnor, "Incentives, Commitments, and Habit Formation in Exercise: Evidence from a Field Experiment with Workers at a Fortune 500 Company," *American Economic Journal: Applied Economics* 7, no. 3 (2015): 51–84, DOI:10.1257/app.20130327.

75 lose more weight: Leslie K. John, George Loewenstein, Andrea B. Troxel, Laurie Norton, Jennifer E. Fassbender, and Kevin G. Volpp, "Financial Incentives for Extended Weight Loss: A Randomized, Controlled Trial," *Journal of General Internal Medicine* 26, no. 6 (2011): 621–26, DOI:10.1007/s11606-010-1628-y.

75 buy healthier groceries: Janet Schwartz, Daniel Mochon, Lauren Wyper, Josiase Maroba, Deepak Patel, and Dan Ariely, "Healthier by Precommitment," *Psychological Science* 25, no. 2 (2014): 538–46, DOI:10.1177/0956797613510950.

76 American adults receive: A. Mark Fendrick, Arnold S. Monto, Brian Nightengale, and Matthew Sarnes, "The Economic Burden of Non-Influenza-Related Viral Respiratory Tract Infection in the United States," *Archives of Internal Medicine* 163, no. 4 (2003): 487–94, DOI:10.1001/archinte.163.4.487.

77 asked doctors to sign: Daniella Meeker, Tara K. Knight, Mark W. Friedberg, Jeffrey A. Linder, Noah J. Goldstein, Craig R. Fox, Alan Rothfeld, Guillermo Diaz, and Jason N. Doctor, "Nudging Guideline-Concordant Antibiotic Prescribing: A Randomized Clinical Trial,"

JAMA Internal Medicine 174, no. 3 (2014): 425–31, DOI:10.1001 /jamainternmed.2013.14191.

78 to *hard penalties,* such as: Rogers et al., "Commitment Devices," 2065–66.

78 at odds with yourself: Leon Festinger, *A Theory of Cognitive Dissonance* (Stanford, CA: Stanford University Press, 1962).

79 student of mine: Karen Herrera, telephone conversation with the author, November 22, 2019.

80 thousands of volunteers: Aneesh Rai, Marissa Sharif, Edward Chang, Katherine L. Milkman, and Angela Duckworth, "The Benefits of Specificity and Flexibility on Goal-Directed Behavior over Time" (working paper, 2020).

80 online financial services: Hal Hershfield, Stephen Shu, and Shlomo Benartzi, "Temporal Reframing and Participation in a Savings Program: A Field Experiment," *Marketing Science* 39, no. 6 (2020): 1033–1201, DOI:10.1287/mksc.2019.1177.

81 The self-help industry is estimated: Marshall Corvus, "Why the Self-Help Industry Is Dominating the U.S.," Medium, February 24, 2019, accessed July 26, 2019, https://medium.com/s/story/no-please-help -yourself-981058f3b7cf.

82 The theory is: Ted O'Donoghue and Matthew Rabin, "Doing It Now or Later," *American Economic Review* 89, no. 1 (1999): 103–24, DOI:10.1257/aer.89.1.103.

83 Dan and Klaus showed: Ariely and Wertenbroch, "Procrastination, Deadlines, and Performance," 219–24.

84 encourage its customers: Hengchen Dai, David Mao, Kevin G. Volpp, Heather E. Pearce, Michael J. Relish, Victor F. Lawnicki, and Katherine L. Milkman, "The Effect of Interactive Reminders on Medication Adherence: A Randomized Trial," *Preventive Medicine* 103 (October 2017): 98–102, DOI:10.1016/j.ypmed.2017.07.019.

CHAPTER 4: FORGETFULNESS

87 In a typical year: "Disease Burden of Influenza," Centers for Disease Control and Prevention, updated October 1, 2020, accessed October 5, 2020, www.cdc.gov/flu/about/burden/index.html.

87 **but in 2009:** "The 2009 H1N1 Pandemic: Summary Highlights, April 2009–April 2010," Centers for Disease Control and Prevention, updated June 16, 2010, accessed October 2, 2020, www.cdc.gov/h1n1 flu/cdcresponse.htm.

87 **far deadlier situation:** Giuliana Viglione, "How Many People Has the Coronavirus Killed?" *Nature*, September 1, 2020, accessed October 2, 2020, www.nature.com/articles/d41586-020-02497-w.

88 **30 percent of employees:** Prashant Srivastava, conversation with the author, September 2009.

89 **the Dow Jones Industrial Average:** "Dow Jones Industrial Average, June 2007 to June 2008," *Wall Street Journal*, accessed February 12, 2020, www.wsj.com/market-data/quotes/index/DJIA/historical-prices.

89 **for the first time since 1952:** Andrew Glass, "Barack Obama Defeats John McCain, November 4, 2008," *Politico,* November 4, 2015, accessed October 8, 2020, www.politico.com/story/2015/11/this-day-in-politics-nov-4-2008-215394.

89 **Democratic nominee, Barack Obama:** Michael Cooper and Dalia Sussman, "McCain and Obama Neck and Neck, Poll Shows," *New York Times*, August 21, 2008, accessed October 2, 2020, www.nytimes.com/2008/08/21/world/americas/21iht-poll.4.15519735.html.

89 **the peculiar rules:** "What Is the Electoral College?" National Archives, last reviewed December 23, 2019, accessed March 30, 2020, www.archives.gov/electoral-college/about.

89 **watching Al Gore lose:** Federal Elections Commission, "2000 Presidential General Election Results," updated December 2001, accessed October 6, 2020, https://web.archive.org/web/20120912083944/http://www.fec.gov/pubrec/2000presgeresults.htm.

89 **fewer than 60 percent:** Drew DeSilver, "U.S. Trails Most Developed Countries in Voter Turnout," Pew Research Center, May 21, 2018, www.pewresearch.org/fact-tank/2018/05/21/u-s-voter-turnout-trails-most-developed-countries.

90 **in one election:** Todd Rogers and Masahiko Aida, "Vote Self-Prediction Hardly Predicts Who Will Vote, and Is (Misleadingly) Unbiased," *American Politics Research* 42, no. 3 (September 2013): 503–28, DOI:10.1177/1532673X13496453.

91 **In fact, evidence suggests that:** Peter Gollwitzer, Frank Wieber, Andrea L. Myers, and Sean M. McCrae, "How to Maximize Implementation Intention Effects," *Then a Miracle Occurs: Focusing on Behavior*

in Social Psychological Theory and Research, ed. Christopher R. Agnew (New York: Oxford University Press, 2009): 137–67.

91 **"I forgot" is:** Todd Rogers, email with the author, August 8, 2019.

91 **a friend of mine:** Judy Chevalier, email with the author, September 12, 2019.

92 **average adult forgets:** "Adults Forget Three Things a Day, Research Finds," *Telegraph,* July 23, 2009, www.telegraph.co.uk/news/uknews /5891701/Adults-forget-three-things-a-day-research-finds.html.

92 **Hermann Ebbinghaus demonstrated:** Hermann Ebbinghaus, *Memory: A Contribution to Experimental Psychology,* trans. H. A. Ruger and C. E. Bussenius (New York: Teachers College, Columbia University, 1913/1885).

92 **This basic pattern has also:** Lee Averell and Andrew Heathcote, "The Form of the Forgetting Curve and the Fate of Memories," *Journal of Mathematical Psychology* 55, no. 1 (February 2011): 25–35, DOI:10.1016/j.jmp.2010.08.009.

93 **"Did one of us goof?":** Dean Karlan, email to the author, April 1, 2019.

93 **Reminding people—by mail:** Peter G. Szilagyi, Clayton Bordley, Julie C. Vann, Ann Chelminksi, Ronald M. Kraus, Peter A. Margolis, and Lance Rodewald. "Effect of Patient Reminder/Recall Interventions on Immunization Rates: A Review," *Journal of the American Medical Association* 284, no. 14 (November 2000): 1820–27, DOI:10.1001 /jama.284.14.1820.

93 **reduces flake out:** Peter A. Briss, Lance E. Rodewald, Alan Hinman, Sergine Ndiaye, and Sheree M. Williams, "Reviews of Evidence Regarding Interventions to Improve Vaccination Coverage in Children, Adolescents, and Adults," *American Journal of Preventive Medicine* 18, no. 1 (January 2000): 97–140, DOI:10.1016/S0749-3797 (99)00118-X.

93 **in low-turnout elections, reminders sent:** Alan S. Gerber, Donald P. Green, and Christopher Larimer, "Social Pressure and Voter Turnout: Evidence from a Large-Scale Field Experiment," *American Political Science Review* 102, no. 1 (February 2008): 33–48. DOI:10.1017 /S000305540808009X.

93 **studies run with banks:** Dean Karlan, Margaret McConnell, Sendhil Mullainathan, and Jonathan Zinman, "Getting to the Top of Mind: How Reminders Increase Saving," *Management Science* 62, no. 12 (December 2016): 3393–3411, DOI:10.1287/mnsc.2015.2296.

94 **involved reminding drivers:** John Austin, Sigurdur O. Sigurdsson, and Yonata S. Rubin. "An Examination of the Effects of Delayed Versus Immediate Prompts on Safety Belt Use," *Environment and Behavior* 38, no. 1 (January 2006): 140–49. DOI:10.1177/0013916505276744.

96 **The study's authors asked:** Peter Gollwitzer and Veronika Brandstatter, "Implementation Intentions and Effective Goal Pursuit," *Journal of Personality and Social Psychology* 73, no. 3 (July 1997): 186–99, DOI:10.1037/0022-3514.73.1.186.

98 **a person can detect:** Peter Gollwitzer, "Implementations Intentions: Strong Effects of Simple Plans," *American Psychologist* 54, no. 7 (1999): 493–503, DOI:10.1037/0003-066X.54.7.493.

98 **The more we engage:** Douglas Hintzman, "Repetition and Memory," *Psychology of Learning and Motivation* 10 (1976): 47–91, DOI:10 .1016/S0079-7421(08)60464-8.

99 **the power of taste:** Marcel Proust, *In Search of Lost Time*, trans. John Sturrock (London: Penguin, 2003).

100 **The research assistants:** Todd Rogers and Katherine L. Milkman, "Reminders through Association," *Psychological Science* 27, no. 7 (May 2016): 973–86, DOI:10.1177/0956797616643071.

101 **written in the 80s BC:** Unknown, *Rhetorica ad Herennium* (London: Loeb Classic Library, 1954), accessed June 24, 2020, http://penelope .uchicago.edu/Thayer/E/Roman/Texts/Rhetorica_ad_Herennium /1*.html.

101 **using this technique:** Jennifer McCabe, "Location, Location, Location! Demonstrating the Mnemonic Benefit of the Method of Loci," *Teaching of Psychology* 42, no. 2 (February 2015): 169–73, DOI:10 .1177/0098628315573143.

102 **This process unfolds:** Tom Ireland, "'Hello, Can We Count on Your Vote?' How I Hit the Phones for Three Different Parties," *The Guardian*, May 6, 2015, accessed October 2, 2020, www.theguardian.com /politics/2015/may/06/hello-can-we-count-your-vote-phone-canvass ing-for-three-parties-election.

102 **from Canada to:** "Phone Calls from Political Parties and Candidates," Canadian Radio-television and Telecommunications Commission, modified April 3, 2020, accessed October 2, 2020, https://crtc.gc.ca /eng/phone/rce-vcr/phone.htm.

102 **to India, and:** Vindu Goel and Suhasini Raj, "In 'Digital India,' Government Hands Out Free Phones to Win Votes," *New York Times*,

November 18, 2018, accessed October 2, 2020, www.nytimes.com /2018/11/18/technology/india-government-free-phones-election.html.

102 **from Norway to:** Johannes Bergh, Dag Arne Christensen, and Richard E. Matland, "When Is a Reminder Enough? Text Message Voter Mobilization in a European Context," *Political Behavior* (2019), DOI:10.1007 /s11109-019-09578-1.

102 **Norway to Australia:** "Political Calls You Might Receive," Australian Communications and Media Authority, updated January 29, 2018, accessed October 2, 2020, www.donotcall.gov.au/consumers/consumer -overview/political-calls-you-might-receive.

102 **By mid-2008:** Todd Rogers, telephone conversation with the author, July 26, 2019.

103 **a voter call script:** David Nickerson and Todd Rogers, "Do You Have A Voting Plan? Implementation Intentions, Voter Turnout, and Organic Plan Making," *Psychological Science* 21, no. 2 (February 2010): 194–99, DOI:10.1177/0956797609359326.

106 **I worked with a team:** Katherine L. Milkman, John Beshears, James J. Choi, David Laibson, and Brigitte C. Madrian, "Using Implementation Intentions Prompts to Enhance Influenza Vaccination Rates," *Proceedings of the National Academy of Sciences* 108, no. 26 (June 2011): 10415–20, DOI:10.1073/pnas.1103170108.

108 **same kinds of planning prompts:** Katherine L. Milkman, John Beshears, James J. Choi, David Laibson, Brigitte C. Madrian, "Planning Prompts as a Means of Increasing Preventative Screening Rates," *Preventive Medicine* 56, no. 1 (January 2013): 92–93, DOI:10.1016/j.ypmed .2012.10.021.

108 **my friend Jason:** Jason Riis, conversation with the author, Philadelphia, October 16, 2019.

109 **Lloyd declared himself:** Lloyd Thomas, conversation with the author, London, June 27, 2019.

110 **someone isn't interested:** Paschal Sheeran, Thomas L. Webb, and Peter M. Gollwitzer, "The Interplay between Goal Intentions and Implementation Intention," *Personality and Social Psychology Bulletin* 31, no.1 (January 2005): 87–98, DOI:10.1177/0146167204271308.

111 **you can overdo:** Amy N. Dalton and Stephen A. Spiller, "Too Much of a Good Thing: The Benefits of Implementation Intentions Depend on the Number of Goals," *Journal of Consumer Research* 39, no. 3 (October 2012): 600–14, DOI:10.1086/664500.

112 his book *The Checklist Manifesto*: Atul Gawande, *The Checklist Manifesto* (New York: Macmillan, 2010).

112 cutting complications and mortality rates: Alex B. Haynes, Thomas G. Weiser, William R. Berry et al., "A Surgical Safety Checklist to Reduce Morbidity and Mortality in a Global Population," *New England Journal of Medicine* 360, no. 5 (2009): 491–99, DOI:10.1056/ NEJMsa0810119.

112 checklists to auto mechanics: Kirabo Jackson and Henry Schneider, "Checklists and Work Behavior: A Field Experiment," *American Economic Journal: Applied Economics* 7, no. 4 (October 2015): 136–68, DOI:10.1257/app.20140044.

112 Todd told me: Todd Rogers, telephone conversation with the author, July 26, 2019.

112 the company has made: Prashant Srivastava, telephone conversation with the author, July 26, 2019.

CHAPTER 5: LAZINESS

117 "What in the world happened?": Steve Honeywell, telephone conversation with the author, December 18, 2019.

117 I first heard the story: Mitesh Patel, lecture at Wharton School at University of Pennsylvania, April 11, 2019.

118 Only 75 percent: Mitesh S. Patel, Susan C. Day, Scott D. Halpern, C. William Hanson, Joseph R. Martinez, Steven Honeywell, and Kevin G. Volpp, "Generic Medication Prescription Rates after Health System–Wide Redesign of Default Options within the Electronic Health Record," *JAMA Internal Medicine* 176, no. 6 (2016): 847–48, DOI:10.1001/jamainternmed.2016.1691.

119 "The Little Red Hen": *The Little Red Hen*, ed. Diane Muldrow (New York: Golden Books, 1954).

119 "The Ant and the Grasshopper": Aesop, "The Ant and the Grasshopper," *Aesop's Fables*, 1867, Lit2Go, accessed October 5, 2020, https:// etc.usf.edu/lit2go/35/aesops-fables/366/-the-ant-and-the-grasshopper.

119 As Herbert Simon: Herbert Simon, *Administrative Behavior: A Study of Decision-Making Processes in Administrative Organizations* (New York: Free Press, 1945), 120.

120 a routine system upgrade: Patel, lecture.

121 Penn Medicine "Nudge Unit": "The Nudge Unit," Penn Medicine, accessed October 5, 2020, https://nudgeunit.upenn.edu.

121 *Nudging* is a term: Richard Thaler and Cass Sunstein, *Nudge* (New Haven, CT: Yale University Press, 2008).

121 famous 2001 study: Brigitte C. Madrian and Dennis F. Shea, "The Power of Suggestion: Inertia in 401(k) Participation and Savings Behavior," *Quarterly Journal of Economics* 116, no. 4 (2001): 1149–87, DOI:10.2139/ssrn.223635.

122 reduce the overprescription: M. Kit Delgado, Francis S. Shofer, Mitesh S. Patel et al., "Association between Electronic Medical Record Implementation of Default Opioid Prescription Quantities and Prescribing Behavior in Two Emergency Departments," *Journal of General Internal Medicine* 33, no. 4 (2018): 409–11, DOI:10.1007/s11606-017-4286-5.

122 limit children's soda: John Peters, Jimikaye Beck, Jan Lande, Zhaoxing Pan, Michelle Cardel, Keith Ayoob, and James O. Hill, "Using Healthy Defaults in Walt Disney World Restaurants to Improve Nutritional Choices," *Journal of the Association for Consumer Research* 1, no. 1 (2016): 92–103, DOI:10.1086/684364.

122 boost flu vaccination rates: Gretchen B. Chapman, Meng Li, Helen Colby, and Haewon Yoon, "Opting In vs Opting Out of Influenza Vaccination," *Journal of the American Medical Association* 304, no. 1 (2010): 43–44. DOI:10.1001/jama.2010.892.

122 raise tips on taxi rides: Kareem Haggag and Giovanni Paci, "Default Tips," *American Economic Journal: Applied Economics* 6, no. 3 (July 2014): 1–19, DOI:10.1257/app.6.3.1.

123 "Everything inside had fallen": Katy Milkman, "Creatures of Habit," *Choiceology*, November 18, 2019, accessed December 18, 2019, www .schwab.com/resource-center/insights/content/choiceology-sea son-4-episode-6.

123 a behavioral side effect: George F. Loewenstein, Elke U. Weber, Christopher K. Hsee, and Ned Welch, "Risk as Feelings," *Psychological Bulletin* 127, no. 2 (March 2001): 267–86, DOI:10.1037/0033-2909 .127.2.267.

123 Neuroscience research shows: Wendy Wood and David Neal, "A New Look at Habits and the Habit-Goal Interference," *Psychological Review* 114, no. 4 (October 2007): 843–63, DOI:10.1037/0033-295X.114.4.843.

125 When behavioral scientists: Milkman, "Creatures of Habit."

125 animals would learn: B. F. Skinner, "Operant Behavior," *American Psychologist* 18, no. 8 (1963): 503–15, DOI:10.1037/h0045185.

126 the same approach that: Gary Charness and Uri Gneezy, "Incentives to Exercise," *Econometrica* 77, no. 3 (2009): 909–31, DOI:10.3982 /ECTA7416.

127 Charles Duhigg's *The Power of Habit*: Charles Duhigg, *The Power of Habit* (New York: Random House, 2012).

127 James Clear's *Atomic Habits*: James Clear, *Atomic Habits* (New York: Avery, Penguin Random House, 2018).

127 positive habits are key: Brian M. Galla and Angela L. Duckworth, "More than Resisting Temptation: Beneficial Habits Mediate the Relationship between Self-Control and Positive Life Outcomes," *Journal of Personality and Social Psychology* 109, no. 3 (2015): 508–25, DOI:10.1037/pspp0000026.

129 healthier employees are happier: Ian Larkin Timothy and Lamar Pierce, "Doing Well by Making Well: The Impact of Corporate Wellness Programs on Employee Productivity," *Management Science* 64, no. 11 (June 2018): 4967–87, DOI:10.2139/ssrn.2811785.

131 Research also demonstrates: Taylor L. Brooks, Howard Leventhal, Michael S. Wolf, Rachel O'Conor, Jose Morillo, Melissa Martynenko, Juan P. Wisnivesky, and Alex D. Federman, "Strategies Used by Older Adults with Asthma for Adherence to Inhaled Corticosteroids," *Journal of General Internal Medicine* 29, no. 11 (2014): 1506–12, DOI:10 .1007/s11606-014-2940-8.

131 gym goers report: Karyn Tappe, Ellen Tarves, Jayme Oltarzewski, and Deirdra Frum, "Habit Formation among Regular Exercisers at Fitness Centers: An Exploratory Study," *Journal of Physical Activity and Health* 10, no. 4 (2013): 607–13, DOI:10.1123/jpah.10.4.607.

131 study about popcorn consumption: David T. Neal, Wendy Wood, Mengju Wu, and David Kurlander, "The Pull of the Past," *Personality and Social Psychology Bulletin* 37, no. 11 (2011): 1428–37, DOI:10 .1177/0146167211419863.

132 Wendy told me: Milkman, "Creatures of Habit."

132 react very differently: Shepard Siegel, Riley E. Hinson, Marvin D. Krank, and Jane McCully, "Heroin Overdose Death: Contribution of Drug-Associated Environmental Cues," *Science* 216, no. 4544 (1982): 436–37, DOI:10.1126/science.7200260.

133 The study we ran involved: John Beshears, Hae Nim Lee, Katherine L. Milkman, and Rob Mislavsky, "Creating Exercise Habits Using Incentives: The Trade-Off between Flexibility and Routinization," *Management Science* (forthcoming).

137 **in his late teens:** Walter Isaacson, *Benjamin Franklin: An American Life* (New York: Simon & Schuster, 2003), 43–44.

137 **comedian Jerry Seinfeld:** Gina Trapani, "Jerry Seinfeld's Productivity Secret," *Lifehacker,* July 24, 2007, accessed July 24, 2019, https://life hacker.com/jerry-seinfelds-productivity-secret-281626.

138 **Research suggests that:** Lora E. Burke et al., "Self-Monitoring in Weight Loss: A Systematic Review of the Literature," *Journal of the American Dietetic Association* 111, no. 1 (2011): 92–102, DOI:10.1016 /j.jada.2010.10.008.

138 **that anything more than a short lapse:** Jackie Silverman and Alixandra Barasch, "On or Off Track: How (Broken) Streaks Affect Consumer Decisions" (working paper, 2020).

140 **kick-start a flossing habit:** Gaby Judah, Benjamin Gardner, and Robert Aunger, "Forming a Flossing Habit: An Exploratory Study of the Psychological Determinants of Habit Formation," *British Journal of Health Psychology* 18, no. 2 (2013): 338–53, DOI:10.1111/j.2044 -8287.2012.02086.x.

CHAPTER 6: CONFIDENCE

143 **"I'll never get it published":** Katy Milkman in conversation with Max Bazerman, Boston, MA, 2007.

145 **average mental health metrics:** Paul Barreira, Matthew Basilico, and Valentin Bolotnyy, "Graduate Student Mental Health: Lessons from American Economics Departments" (working paper, 2018), https:// scholar.harvard.edu/files/bolotnyy/files/bbb_mentalhealth_paper.pdf.

145 **a 2012 email:** Katy Milkman, email to Max Bazerman, January 8, 2012.

145 **"students who range":** Max Bazerman, email with the author, January 13, 2012.

147 **As a PhD student in psychology:** Lauren Eskreis-Winkler, telephone conversation with the author, November 1, 2019.

147 **surveyed Americans struggling:** Katy Milkman, "Your Own Advice," *Choiceology,* October 7, 2019, accessed December 20, 2019, www.sch wab.com/resource-center/insights/content/choiceology-season-4 -episode-3.

148 **has called "a lack of self-efficacy":** Albert Bandura, "Self-Efficacy: Toward a Unifying Theory of Behavioral Change," *Psychological Review* 84, no. 2 (1977): 191, DOI:10.1037/0033-295X.84.2.191.

148 **person's confidence in their ability:** Michael P. Carey and Andrew D. Forsyth, "Teaching Tip Sheet: Self-Efficacy," *American Psychological Association* (2009), accessed June 25, 2020, www.apa.org/pi/aids /resources/education/self-efficacy.

148 **when we don't believe:** Bandura, "Self-Efficacy," 191.

148 **trying to lose weight:** Jennifer A. Linde, Alexander J. Rothman, Austin S. Baldwin, and Robert W. Jeffery, "The Impact of Self-Efficacy on Behavior Change and Weight Change among Overweight Participants in a Weight Loss Trial," *Health Psychology* 25, no. 3 (2006): 282–91, DOI:10.1037/0278-6133.25.3.282.

148 **science and engineering undergraduates:** Robert W. Lent, Steven D. Brown, and Kevin C. Larkin, "Relation of Self-Efficacy Expectations to Academic Achievement and Persistence," *Journal of Counseling Psychology* 31, no. 3 (1984): 356–62, DOI:10.1037/0022-0167.31 .3.356.

149 **quick to infer:** Craig R. M. McKenzie, Michael J. Liersch, and Stacey R. Finkelstein, "Recommendations Implicit in Policy Defaults," *Psychological Science* 17, no. 5 (May 2006): 414–20, DOI:10.1111/j.1467 -9280.2006.01721.x.

149 **most people predicted:** Lauren Eskreis-Winkler, Ayelet Fishbach, and Angela L. Duckworth, "Dear Abby: Should I Give Advice or Receive It?" *Psychological Science* 29, no. 11 (2018): 1797–806, DOI:10.1177 /0956797618795472.

150 **massive experiment aimed:** Lauren Eskreis-Winkler, Katherine L. Milkman, Dena M. Gromet, and Angela L. Duckworth, "A Large-Scale Field Experiment Shows Giving Advice Improves Academic Outcomes for the Advisor," *Proceedings of the National Academy of Sciences* 116, no. 30 (2019): 14808–10, DOI:10.1073/pnas.1908779116.

151-152 **called the "saying-is-believing effect":** E. Aronson, "The Power of Self-Persuasion." *American Psychologist* 54, no. 11, (1999): 875–84, DOI:10 .1037/h0088188.

152 **the legendary drummer:** Milkman, "Your Own Advice."

153 **women tend to bear:** Linda Babcock, Maria P. Recalde, Lise Vesterlund, and Laurie Weingart, "Gender Differences in Accepting and Receiving Requests for Tasks with Low Promotability," *American Economic Review* 107, no. 3 (2017): 714–47, DOI:10.1257/aer.20 141734.

154 **becoming a sponsor:** Alcoholics Anonymous General Service Conference, *Questions & Answers on Sponsorship*, Alcoholics Anonymous World Services, Inc., 2017, accessed October 5, 2020, www.aa.org /assets/en_us/p-15_Q&AonSpon.pdf.

154 **Mentoring programs in companies:** Yang Song, George Loewenstein, and Yaojiang Shi, "Heterogeneous Effects of Peer Tutoring: Evidence from Rural Chinese Middle Schools," *Research in Economics* 72, no. 1 (2018): 33–48, DOI:10.1016/j.rie.2017.05.002.

155 **housekeepers who volunteered:** Alia J. Crum and Ellen J. Langer, "Mind-Set Matters: Exercise and the Placebo Effect," *Psychological Science* 18, no. 2 (2007): 165–71, DOI:10.1111/j.1467-9280.2007 .01867.x.

156 **a useless sugar pill:** Anton de Craen, Ted Kaptchuk, Jan Tijssen, and J. Kleijnen, "Placebos and Placebo Effects in Medicine: Historical Overview," *Journal of the Royal Society of Medicine* 92, no. 10 (October 1999): 511–15, DOI:10.1177/014107689909201005.

157 **attributing the butterflies:** Alison Wood Brooks, "Get Excited: Reappraising Pre-Performance Anxiety as Excitement," *Journal of Experimental Psychology: General* 143, no. 3 (2014): 1144, DOI:10.1037 /a0035325.

157 **believing that people expect:** Catherine Good, Joshua Aronson, and Michael Inzlicht, "Improving Adolescents' Standardized Test Performance: An Intervention to Reduce the Effects of Stereotype Threat," *Journal of Applied Developmental Psychology* 24, no. 6 (2003): 645–62, DOI:10.1016/j.appdev.2003.09.002.

157 **in four key ways:** Alia Crum, interview with the author, June 16, 2020.

157 **generates positive feelings:** Samantha Dockray and Andrew Steptoe, "Positive Affect and Psychobiological Processes," *Neuroscience and Biobehavioral Reviews* 35, no. 1 (September 2010): 69–75, DOI:10 .1016/j.neubiorev.2010.01.006.

158 **they produced less:** Alia J. Crum, William R. Corbin, Kelly D. Brownwell, and Peter Salovey, "Mind over Milkshakes: Mindsets, Not Just Nutrients, Determine Ghrelin Response," *Health Psychology* 30, no. 4 (2011): 424–29, DOI:10.1037/a0023467.

158 **power of our beliefs:** David Mikkelson, "The Unsolvable Math Problem," Snopes, December 4, 1996, accessed December 12, 2019, www .snopes.com/fact-check/the-unsolvable-math-problem.

159 **the legendary CEO:** Jack and Suzy Welch, "Are Leaders Born or Made? Here's What's Coachable—and What's Definitely Not," LinkedIn, May 1, 2016, accessed December 20, 2019, www.linkedin .com/pulse/leaders-born-made-heres-whats-coachable-definitely-jack-welch.

160 **2014 Super Bowl:** Matthew Futterman, "Seattle Seahawks Coach Pete Carroll Wants to Change Your Life," *Chicago Tribune*, January 10, 2020, accessed November 20, 2019, www.chicagotribune.com/sports /national-sports/sns-nyt-seattle-seahawks-pete-carroll-wants-change -your-life-20200110-v6movm4yufgkdb67cz3m2qx6ia-story.html.

160 **the aptly named:** Winona Cochran and Abraham Tesser, "The 'What the Hell' Effect: Some Effects of Goal Proximity and Goal Framing on Performance," *Striving and Feeling: Interactions among Goals, Affect, and Self-Regulation*, eds. Leonard L. Martin and Abraham Tesser (Mahwah, NJ: Lawrence Erlbaum Associates, 1996), 99–120.

161 **Marissa allows herself:** Marissa A. Sharif, email with the author, January 10, 2020.

161 **study involving hundreds:** Marissa A. Sharif and Suzanne B. Shu, "The Benefits of Emergency Reserves: Greater Preference and Persistence for Goals That Have Slack with a Cost," *Journal of Marketing Research* 54, no. 3 (June 2017): 495–509, DOI:10.1509/jmr.15.0231.

163 **we interpret failure has:** Carol S. Dweck, *Mindset: The New Psychology of Success*, updated edition (New York: Random House, 2016).

163 **having a "growth mind-set":** Dweck, *Mindset*.

163 **thousands of high school freshmen:** David S. Yeager, Paul Hanselman, Gregory M. Walton et al., "A National Experiment Reveals Where a Growth Mindset Improves Achievement," *Nature* 573, no. 7774 (2019): 364–69, DOI:10.1038/s41586-019-1466-y.

164 **Developing a growth mind-set:** Harvard Business Review Staff, "How Companies Can Profit from a 'Growth Mindset,'" *Harvard Business Review*, November 2014, accessed October 6, 2020, https://hbr.org /2014/11/how-companies-can-profit-from-a-growth-mindset.

164 **Israelis and Palestinians:** Carol S. Dweck, "Mindsets and Human Nature: Promoting Change in the Middle East, the Schoolyard, the Racial Divide, and Willpower," *American Psychologist* 67, no. 8 (2012): 614–22, DOI:10.1037/a0029783.

164 **engaging in self-affirmation:** Claude M. Steele, "The Psychology of Self-Affirmation: Sustaining the Integrity of the Self," *Advances in*

Experimental Social Psychology 21, no. 2 (1988): 261–302, DOI: 10.1016/S0065-2601(08)60229-4.

164 **improve the decision quality:** Crystal C. Hall, Jiaying Zhao, and Eldar Shafir, "Self-Affirmation among the Poor," *Psychological Science* 25, no. 2 (2013): 619–25, DOI:10.1177/0956797613510949.

165 **famously declared overconfidence:** David Shariatmadari, "Daniel Kahneman: 'What would I eliminate if I had a magic wand? Overconfidence,'" *The Guardian*, July 18, 2015, accessed October 6, 2020, www.theguardian.com/books/2015/jul/18/daniel-kahneman-books -interview.

166 **way we compliment people:** Claudia A. Mueller and Carol S. Dweck, "Praise for Intelligence Can Undermine Children's Motivation and Performance," *Journal of Personality and Social Psychology* 75, no. 1 (1998): 33–52, DOI:10.1037/0022-3514.75.1.33.

CHAPTER 7: CONFORMITY

169 **Carrell felt anxious:** Scott Carrell, telephone conversation with the author, November 14, 2019.

172 **norms create pressure:** Noah J. Goldstein and Robert B. Cialdini, "Using Social Norms as a Lever of Social Influence," *The Science of Social Influence: Advances and Future Progress* (2007): 167–92.

173 **To test his hunch:** Scott E. Carrell, Richard L. Fullerton, and James E. West, "Does Your Cohort Matter? Measuring Peer Effects in College Achievement," *Journal of Labor Economics* 27, no. 3 (July 2009): 439–64, DOI:10.1086/600143.

173 **when your peers attend:** Esther Duflo and Emmanuel Saez, "The Role of Information and Social Interactions in Retirement Plan Decisions: Evidence from a Randomized Experiment," *Quarterly Journal of Economics* 118, no. 3 (2003): 815–42, DOI:10.1162/00335530360698432.

173 **Everything from our grades:** Bruce Sacerdote, "Peer Effects with Random Assignment: Results for Dartmouth Roommates," *Quarterly Journal of Economics* 116, no. 2 (2001): 681–704, DOI:10.1162/0033 5530151144131.

173 **to our careers:** Lucas C. Coffman, Clayton R. Featherstone, and Judd B. Kessler, "Can Social Information Affect What Job You Choose and Keep?" *American Economic Journal: Applied Economics* 9, no. 1 (2017): 96–117, DOI:10.1257/app.20140468.

173 **to our financial decisions:** Duflo and Saez, "The Role of Information," 815–42.

174 **Kassie Brabaw experienced:** Kassie Brabaw, conversation with the author, Philadelphia, PA, June 2019.

176 **"false consensus effect":** Lee Ross, David Greene, and Pamela House, "The 'False Consensus Effect': An Egocentric Bias in Social Perception and Attribution Processes," *Journal of Experimental Social Psychology* 13, no. 3 (1977): 279–301, DOI:10.1016/0022-1031(77)90049-x.

176 **two studies led:** Katie S. Mehr, Amanda E. Geiser, Katherine L. Milkman, and Angela L. Duckworth, "Copy-Paste Prompts: A New Nudge to Promote Goal Achievement," *Journal of the Association for Consumer Research* 5, no. 3 (2020): 329–334, DOI:10.1086/708880.

177 **more influenced by observation:** F. Marijn Stok, Denise T. D. de Ridder, Emely de Vet, and John B. F. de Wit, "Don't Tell Me What I Should Do, but What Others Do: The Influence of Descriptive and Injunctive Peer Norms on Fruit Consumption in Adolescents," *British Journal of Health Psychology* 19, no. 1 (2014): 52–64, DOI:10.1111/bjhp.12030.

179 **persuade more guests:** Noah J. Goldstein, Robert B. Cialdini, and Vladas Griskevicius, "A Room with a Viewpoint: Using Social Norms to Motivate Environmental Conservation in Hotels," *Journal of Consumer Research* 35, no. 3 (March 2008): 472–82, DOI:10.1086/586910.

179 **get-out-the-vote experiment:** Robert M. Bond, Christopher J. Fariss, Jason J. Jones, Adam D. I. Kramer, Cameron Marlow, Jaime E. Settle, and James H. Fowler, "A 61-Million-Person Experiment in Social Influence and Political Mobilization," *Nature* 489 (September 2012): 295–98, DOI:10.1038/nature11421.

180 **research on the sway:** Solomon E. Asch, "Opinions and Social Pressure," *Scientific American* 193, no. 5 (November 1955): 17–26, DOI:10.1038/scientificamerican1155-31.

180 **that social pressure can be used:** Stanley Milgram, "Behavioral Study of Obedience," *Journal of Abnormal and Social Psychology* 67, no. 4 (October 1963): 371–78, DOI:10.1037/h0040525.

180 **coercive uses of social pressure:** Stanley Milgram, "Some Conditions of Obedience and Disobedience to Authority," *Human Relations* 18, no. 1 (1965): 57–76, DOI:10.1177/001872676501800105.

182 **the top brass quickly gave:** Scott E. Carrell, Bruce I. Sacerdote, and James E. West, "From Natural Variation to Optimal Policy? The

Importance of Endogenous Peer Group Formation," *Econometrica* 81, no. 3 (May 2013): 855–82, DOI:10.3982/ECTA10168.

183 **My lesson came:** John Beshears, James J. Choi, David Laibson, Brigette C. Madrian, and Katherine L. Milkman, "The Effect of Providing Peer Information on Retirement Savings Decisions," *Journal of Finance* 70, no. 3 (February 2015): 1161–1201, DOI:10.1111/jofi.12258.

184 **Our results made us think:** Cochran and Tesser, "*The 'What the Hell' Effect*," 99–120.

187 **But this message:** Alan S. Gerber, Donald P. Green, and Christopher Larimer, "Social Pressure and Voter Turnout: Evidence from a Large-Scale Field Experiment," *American Political Science Review* 102, no. 1 (February 2008): 33–48, DOI:10.1017/S000305540808009X.

189 **boost sign-ups for a green:** Erez Yoeli, Moshe Hoffman, David G. Rand, and Martin A. Nowak, "Powering Up with Indirect Reciprocity in a Large-Scale Field Experiment," *Proceedings of the National Academy of Sciences* 110, supplement 2 (June 2013): 10424–29, DOI: 10.1073/pnas.1301210110.

190 **Most of us want:** Daniel Sznycer, Laith Al-Shawaf, Yoella Bereby-Meyer et al., "Cross-Cultural Regularities in the Cognitive Architecture of Pride," *Proceedings of the National Academy of Sciences* 114, no. 8 (February 2017): 1874–79, DOI:10.1073/pnas.1614389114.

190 **likely to make donations:** Dean Karlan and Margaret A. McConnell, "Hey Look at Me: The Effect of Giving Circles on Giving," *Journal of Economic Behavior & Organization* 106 (2014): 402–12, DOI:10.1016/j.jebo.2014.06.013.

191 **behavior is merely trending:** Chad R. Mortensen, Rebecca Neel, Robert B. Cialdini, Christine M. Jaeger, Ryan P. Jacobson, and Megan M. Ringel, "Trending Norms: A Lever for Encouraging Behaviors Performed by the Minority," *Social Psychological and Personality Science* 10, no. 2 (December 2017): 201–10, DOI:10.1177/194855061 7734615.

CHAPTER 8: CHANGING FOR GOOD

195 **declared at the same time:** Angela Duckworth, conversation with the author, Philadelphia, PA, 2018.

195 **run a massive experiment:** Katherine L. Milkman et al., "A Mega-Study Approach to Evaluating Interventions" (working paper, 2020).

195 **Roughly half of Americans:** Brian W. Ward, Tainya C. Clarke, Colleen N. Nugent, and Jeannine S. Schiller, "Early Release of Selected Estimates Based on Data From the 2015 National Health Interview Survey," National Center for Health Statistics (2015): 120, www.cdc.gov/nchs/data/nhis/earlyrelease/earlyrelease201605.pdf.

196 **applied behavioral economics:** "Center for Health Incentives and Behavioral Economics," University of Pennsylvania, accessed March 24, 2020. https://chibe.upenn.edu.

197 **"When we diagnose someone":** Kevin Volpp, telephone conversation with the author, 2018.

197 **home-energy reports:** Hunt Allcott and Todd Rogers, "The Short-Run and Long-Run Effects of Behavioral Interventions: Experimental Evidence from Energy Conservation," *The American Economic Review* 104, no. 10 (2014): 3003–7, www.jstor.org/stable/43495312.

199 **Years after beginning:** Karen Herrera, telephone conversation with the author, November 22, 2019.

Index

About the Author

Katy Milkman is the James G. Dinan Professor at the Wharton School of the University of Pennsylvania, host of Charles Schwab's popular behavioral economics podcast *Choiceology*, and the former president of the international Society for Judgment and Decision Making. She is the cofounder and codirector of the Behavior Change for Good Initiative, a research center with the mission of advancing the science of lasting behavior change whose work is being chronicled by *Freakonomics Radio*. Over the course of her career, she has worked with or advised dozens of organizations on how to spur positive change, including Google, the U.S. Department of Defense, the American Red Cross, 24 Hour Fitness, Walmart, and Morningstar. An award-winning scholar and teacher, Katy writes frequently about behavioral science for major media outlets such as *The Washington Post*, *The New York Times*, *The Economist*, *USA Today*, and *Scientific American*. She earned her undergraduate degree from Princeton University, where she studied Operations Research and American Studies (and played varsity tennis), and her PhD from Harvard University, where she studied Computer Science and Business. Katy lives with her husband and son in Philadelphia, Pennsylvania.